Walt Whitman in Fernando Pessoa

Francesca Pasciolla

Critical, Cultural and Communications Press
London
2016

Walt Whitman in Fernando Pessoa
by Francesca Pasciolla

Series: Pessoa Studies, vol. 2.
Works in this series are academically refereed.

The right of Francesca Pasciolla to be identified as author of this work has been asserted by her in accordance with the Copyright, Designs and Patents Act, 1988.

© Francesca Pasciolla, 2016.

All unauthorised reproduction is hereby prohibited. This work is protected by law. It should not be duplicated or distributed, in whole or in part, in soft or hard copy, by any means whatsoever, without the prior and conditional permission of the Publisher, CCC Press.

First published in Great Britain by Critical, Cultural and Communications Press, 2016, with the support of the Instituto Camões.

All rights reserved.

Cover design and illustrations by the author.

The annotations in the hand of Alexander Search and of Fernando Pessoa, respectively, are taken from the margins of the works, including those of and on Walt Whitman, discovered in the personal library of the Portuguese poet.

ISBN 9781905510498

Contents

Foreword	7
Acknowledgments	8
"The only preface needed…"	9
Chapter I: Pessoa, reader of Whitman	14
Chapter II: Whitman, writer of Pessoa	22
Chapter III: Toings and froings	84
Bibliography	127
Index	131

I do not look for a vast audience – for great numbers of endorsers, absorbers – just now, perhaps not even after a while. But here and there, every now and then, one, several, will raise the standard.

Walt Whitman

Ao Roberto V
Imperador da Eterna Juventude

Foreword

For T.S. Eliot, "Immature poets imitate, mature poets steal; bad poets deface what they take, and good poets make it into something better or, at least, something different". For Francesca Pasciolla – is this a revenant F.P.? – mature critics are the issue, anxious to tell us what the later poet would have us know of his (or their, for her principal concern is with Fernando Pessoa, Alexander Search, Alberto Caeiro, Álvaro de Campos) relationships with, attitudes to, uses of, departures from, the "great yawp" precursor. A rigorous evidence-based examination of the much-heralded poet's ever-tantalizing writings – be they poems, polemics or marginalia – is evinced in her refreshingly succinct study. Walt Whitman's discursive (pr)axis is (de)constructed upon Pasciolla's detailed knowledge of the respective texts and of the comparative North American and Portuguese literary and literary-critical contexts. The sub-text of her book, "Let there be commerce between us", taking up on behalf of the celebrated Portuguese masker of poetic personae the challenge of Ezra Pound's "I make a pact with you, Walt Whitman", operates as a welcome, if subtly respectful, corrective to the putatively closed markets and mind-sets that have underpinned so many pronouncements on and about Pessoa; to already, if prematurely, settled academic transactions, not least, for instance, the stubborn identity-chasing, even psychologizing, of notoriously irrepressible heteronymities.

Marcel Grousse

Acknowledgments

The author extends her thanks to the editors of Critical, Cultural and Communications Press, and to the Instituto Camões.

"The only preface needed..."

De resto, o único prefácio de uma obra é o cérebro de quem a lê.[1]
Álvaro de Campos

The purpose of this book is to explore the dynamics that connect two of the most celebrated poets and intriguing literary figures of the nineteenth and twentieth centuries, Walt Whitman and Fernando Pessoa. It focuses in particular on the role of the Portuguese Pessoa as reader of the North American writer, on the lessons he took from *Leaves of Grass* and, finally, on the reworking that he performed on Whitman's legacy. Even to approach the biography of celebrated authors provokes a certain unease and reticence; the sense of circumspection becomes more acute when we confront such a life as that of Pessoa – an anonymous existence lived out between melancholy rented rooms and employment as translator of commercial letters. We shall endeavour, therefore, to keep speculation under control in favour of looking at evidence of the irrefutably crucial poetic relationship.

Eugenio Montale, in "Per Finire", wrote: "Vissi al cinque per cento, non aumentate la dose" ["I lived at five per cent, don't increase the dose"]. Something similar might apply to Pessoa, a Portuguese Bartleby, or another *man* (apparently) *without qualities* who one morning could have woken up as a Gregor Samsa-like beetle. In fact, once we have broken into the hard shell so stubbornly constructed, it becomes obvious that the life of Pessoa was only ostensibly ordinary: he had, indeed, figured in the foremost Portuguese journals of the early twentieth century (*A Águia, Centauro, Portugal Futurista, Presença*, to name but a few), had himself founded at least two (*Orpheu, Athena*), had reinterpreted the Portuguese avant-garde and the European literary tendencies (futurism, cubism and surrealism), and had invented at least three movements through his own efforts (*paulismo, sensacionismo* and *interseccionismo*).

---

[1] ["Besides, the only preface of a work is the brain of whoever reads it".] Draft for the preface of Fernando Pessoa's "Cancioneiro" (Pessoa 1996: 428).

Born in Lisbon in 1888, Fernando Pessoa lost his father when he was just five. When his mother remarried, all the family moved to Durban, South Africa, where the stepfather was the Portuguese consul. For almost ten years, from 1896 to 1905, Pessoa lived in South Africa, where he pursued all his studies in English. On his return to Lisbon, he briefly attempted to continue studying in the Faculty of Arts, but soon gave up. There followed several unsuccessful commercial and publishing ventures.

Such was his life until 8 March 1914, the moment Pessoa declared his "dia triunfal" ["triumphal day"]. This date has come to be regarded as the outset of the so-called heteronymic experience. What happened, or rather, what Pessoa wanted to be persuaded of, was – in prey to a sudden ecstasy of creation – he was inhabited by his "Master", Alberto Caeiro, and then by the latter's disciples Ricardo Reis and Álvaro de Campos.[2] As if "possessed" (if I may use the term) by Alberto Caeiro, the poet had written in a single burst thirty or more poems that would turn out to be *O Guardador de Rebanhos* [*The Keeper of Flocks*]; he would then go back to being himself to compose the six sections of the poem "Chuva oblíqua" and, at length, as Álvaro de Campos, he would write the verses of "Ode Triunfal" ["Triumphal Ode"] (Tabucchi and Lancastre 2007: 133).

It is not my concern here to discuss the plausibility of such a statement. In the last fifty years, the explosion of the heteronyms has been the object of innumerable debates. Whether or not based on purely aesthetic, physiological or psychoanalytical reasons, what matters here is the work's literary value – and this is obviously high, since Pessoa's invisible *côterie* (Tabucchi and Lancastre 2007: 133) is made up of poets, prose writers, philosophers, charade experts, crime novelists, translators, each with his own voice and individual style. There have been some eighty of them counted to date, but in this study of the Pessoa-Whitman relationship we shall focus primarily on Alberto Caeiro, Álvaro de Campos and Alexander Search.

Fernando Pessoa died on 30 November 1935, in Lisbon, from a crisis of the

---

[2] The word "Master" was used by Pessoa in a letter of 13 January 1935 to Adolfo Casais Monteiro. It is generally considered as the letter on the origin of the heteronyms (Tabucchi and Lancastre 2007: 128-136).

liver brought about by alcohol abuse. The previous year, he had published his only volume of verses in Portuguese, *Mensagem* [*Message*], with which he had competed for the prize awarded by the Secretariado de Propaganda Nacional [National Propaganda Secretariat]. After his death, a trunk was discovered containing thousands of writings, orthonymic (that is, overtly by Pessoa himself) and heteronymic, all penned by the Portuguese poet. What had seemed to be a quintessentially banal existence was, at a stroke, revealed to have been an intense and active life, underpinned by the rhythms of feverish writing. In 1945, Ática began to publish the complete works of Pessoa, but the trunk of unpublished texts has not ceased to throw up surprises and challenges to philologists, literary critics and Pessoa enthusiasts throughout the world.

We have hinted but in passing at the heteronym Alexander Search. Although less known (and considered by some to be not really a heteronym, rather a pre-heteronym because he had first appeared prior to the red-letter day of 1914), he divulges a role crucial to our investigations. It is, in fact, as Alexander Search that Pessoa encountered Whitman. In a file signed by Pessoa, we learn that Search was born in Lisbon on the same day as his creator, 13 June 1888; he began to carry on a correspondence with Pessoa in 1899 and from him there remain various poems in English, a story titled *A Very Original Dinner* and many texts, amongst which is a pact with Satan dated 2 October 1907. Yet, what captures our attention most is that, probably in 1906, Search obtained an anthology of poems by Walt Whitman, which makes up part of the personal library of Fernando Pessoa. This curious fact will be further considered in the first chapter. For now, let it suffice to acknowledge the devastating impact that the verses of the American poet appear to have had on the adolescent Pessoa-Search who, let it be recalled, had an added advantage: t(he)y could read Whitman directly in English.

Walt Whitman, "a kosmos, of Manhattan the son,/ Turbulent, fleshy, sensual, eating, drinking and breeding", according to section XXIV of "Song of Myself", was besides anything else a highly captivating figure; in the eyes of the young Portuguese he seems to have had an impact not unlike that of a rock star nowadays. We know that he was born in 1819 in Long Island and that, in contrast to Pessoa, he liked to "dirty his hands": as a boy, he had begun to work as a typographer (he was the *printer's devil*, or an apprentice); for a few years he was an elementary school teacher and then dedicated himself fully to journalism and literature. In 1855, he published the first edition of *Leaves of Grass*: this was a collection of just twelve poems and it appeared without the name of the author. Whitman wanted, however, a photograph of him to be included, wearing a labourer's smock and a hat. What few know is that the title *Leaves of Grass* was a play on words: the term "grass" referred, in the world of publishing, to works of little value, whilst "leaves" served to designate the pages on which such works were printed.

In 1861, with the outbreak of the Civil War, Whitman set off as a freelance journalist. A year later, he transferred to Washington D. C. to tend to his brother, wounded in battle. He worked in the Department of the Interior for eleven years, until he was identified as the author of *Leaves of Grass* – a work regarded by many as "indecent" – and was fired. He settled, therefore, in New Jersey, to assist his dying mother. In 1884, Walt was finally in a position to buy his first house, in Camden, thanks to the growing international success that came to him through his poems. From there he moved but little, not least because of a stroke that left him disabled. He continued, however, to work on his new editions of *Leaves of Grass* (from 1855 to 1891 there were some eight) and on a volume in prose (*Good-Bye, My Fancy*) and his home became a place of pilgrimage for several authors and friends, including Oscar Wilde and Thomas Eakins. The "barbaric yawp" died in 1892, the year in which there appeared the so-called "deathbed edition" of *Leaves of Grass*, that was made up of more or less four hundred poems.[3]

Walt Whitman: who embraced continents; who allowed himself to be absorbed by the worlds that surrounded him and, at the same time, enveloped them within himself; who yielded to the lures of everything external to him; who indulged a pantheism that was both spiritual and material. Fernando Pessoa: the man who observed the world from his window; who showed scant interest in sexuality (his own or that of others),[4] and also wrote of himself, "I

---

[3] It is the "barbaric yawp" Whitman mentions in "Song of Myself".
[4] These words are used by Pessoa in a letter of 11 December 1931 to João Gaspar Simões.

can paint, but I have never painted; I can compose music, but I have never composed" (Pessoa 1996: 15). Whitman and Pessoa: two opposed yet magnetic poles, which interact and mutually attract; two "universal brothers",[5] as Álvaro de Campos would have it, who gave voice to a reality which was transformed into frantic rhythms.

In the twenty-first century, it is still pertinent to look again, and closely, at these two writers, not only as a way of grasping the past (hardly remote), and thereby gain insight into the present, but also because their appeal may be shown to be persistent, their writings revealed as mutually enlightening, as is properly the case with the greatest authors.

In fine, or at the outset, we may listen to Antonio Tabucchi:

Per spiegare Pessoa, e magari anche per neutralizzare l'inquietudine che egli ci comunica, si è parlato di turbe e di traumi, di carenza affettiva, di complesso edipico, di omosessualità rimossa. Forse c'è tutto questo e forse niente di questo: ma non è questo il punto e non è questo che conta. Quello che conta è, come egli ci ha detto, che "la letteratura, come tutta l'arte, è la dimostrazione che la vita non basta". (Tabucchi and Lancastre 2007: 25)[6]

[In order to explain Pessoa, and perhaps also to neutralize the anxiety that he communicates to us, there has been talk of disorders and traumas, of a lack of affection, of an oedipal complex, and of repressed homosexuality. Maybe there is all of this, and maybe there is none of it: but this is not the point, and it is not this that matters. What matters is that, as he himself has told us, "literature, like all art, is the demonstration that life is not enough".]

---

[5] Álvaro de Campos, in the poem "Saudação a Walt Whitman", addresses the American poet by calling him "irmão em Universo" ["Universal brother"].
[6] The original quotation is contained in "Erostratus" and reads thus: "A literatura, como toda a arte, é uma confissão de que a vida não basta".

Chapter I
Pessoa, reader of Whitman

> *Camerado! This is no book;*
> *Who touches this, touches a man...*
> Walt Whitman, "So Long"

> *(I touch your book and dream of our*
> *odyssey in the supermarket and feel absurd)*
> Allen Ginsberg, "A Supermarket in California"

It is often possible to intuit the interests and the preferences, the concerns and the aesthetic leanings of someone simply by glancing quickly at the contents of their bookshelves, without feeling it necessary to open a single volume. Among the 1,311 items of Fernando Pessoa's particular library, there have been discovered four by or on Walt Whitman (Ferrari 2011: 24):

Perry, Bliss. *Walt Whitman: His Life and Work*. London: Archibald Constable, 1906.
Rivers, Walter Courtenay. *Walt Whitman's Anomaly*. London: George Allen, 1913.
Whitman, Walt. *Leaves of Grass*. London: Cassell, 1909.
Whitman, Walt. *Poems*. London: The Masterpiece Library, undated.

Pessoa possessed two poetry anthologies by Whitman. The first one is a relatively old edition of a collection titled simply *Poems by Walt Whitman* (which contains the major part of "Song of Myself"); the second is a more recent edition that contains almost all of *Leaves of Grass*.

We shall concentrate above all on *Poems by Walt Whitman*. While the exact date of publication (probably 1895) is not known, we have reasons to believe that Pessoa came to obtain the book around 1906, the moment that he showed a first glimmer of interest in the American writer, though according to Richard Zenith this interest can be found as early as 1895 (Zenith 2013: 45).

This copy, apparently the first contact Pessoa had with Whitman's poetry, may well have been the only direct access he had until 1916, when he bought a more complete edition of *Leaves of Grass*. An interesting detail associated with *Poems by Walt Whitman* is that it did not "belong" to Pessoa himself, but to his early heteronym Alexander Search; on the first page, we read, indeed, the signature and the monogram, thus:

Detail of the first page of *Poems by Walt Whitman*, with Alexander Search's signature ("A Search") and monogram (AS).

Although this fact is not surprising (until now there are up to at least twenty-five books marked as belonging to the heteronym – volumes in five different languages: English, French, Portuguese, Spanish and Greek) (Ferrari 2011: 36), it can be assumed, however, from the extraordinary number of verses underlined, circled and commented on in the margins, that *Poems by Walt Whitman* was read and reread by Pessoa-Search with particular enthusiasm. The copy looks like a veritable palimpsest, showing stratified comments made by different hands and at different times. It is on this aspect that Patricio Ferrari insists, namely on the fact that the book was enjoyed by two different personalities: first, Alexander Search, for about the first four or five years, until the time of his "disappearance"; second, Fernando Pessoa, who therefore kept it and annotated it until he died.⁷ The last literary works by Search are dated up to 1910 and it is possible that his role as keeper of books ended about then. Four years before "disappearing", Search had written in a notebook of the interest he had in Whitman. Indeed, one of his lists has been found, dated "September, 1906", on which the young heteronym's reading choices appear. Under the letter "T", we can read: "10. Trimble (W[illiam] H[eywood]): 'Walt Whitman and Leaves of Grass'" (Ferrari 2011: 37).

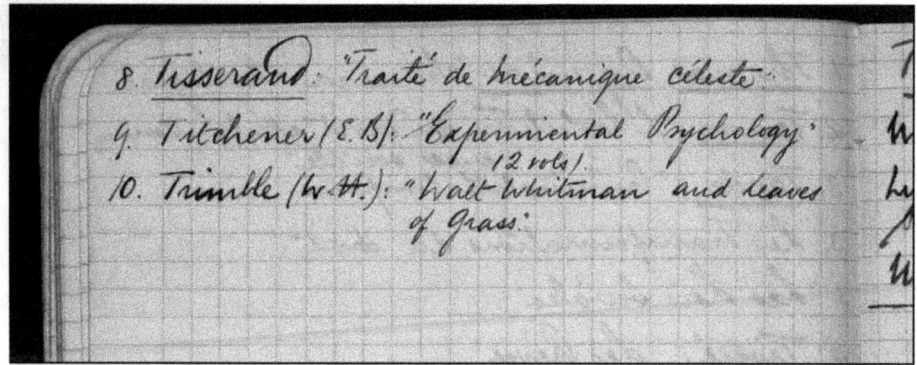

Detail of notebook 144-H.

Turning to *Poems by Walt Whitman*, Patricio Ferrari highlights a further aspect: over a series of verses cited in the introduction, where the poet best expresses his Universalist doctrine, Pessoa had annotated "explanation for Caeiro's".

This discovery would demystify the mythical image of the "dia triunfal" as some ecstatic revelation, revealing how the creation of the heteronymy was really a calculated act. But this is not territory into which we shall venture. For now, we shall continue to follow the traces left by Search (firstly) and by Pessoa (thereafter) on Whitman's books.

From looking at *Poems by Walt Whitman*, another noteworthy element emerges. The cover of the book is full of annotations, left by Pessoa-Search, that render it more like a notepad than an anthology of poetry. One of these

---

⁷ Ferrari makes a distinction between heteronymic and pre-heteronymic figures. Apparently, only Pessoa's pre-heteronyms owned books. Neither Alberto Caeiro nor any other heteronym was a bookkeeper.

notes, the only one written in Portuguese (which stands out amidst so many in English) reads: "Às vezes, numa batalha, não é um que ganha; é o outro que perde" ["At times, in a battle, it is not that someone wins; it is just that the other one loses"], which might be a response to Whitman's verses "[i]t is good to fall, battles are lost in the same spirit in which they are won".[8]

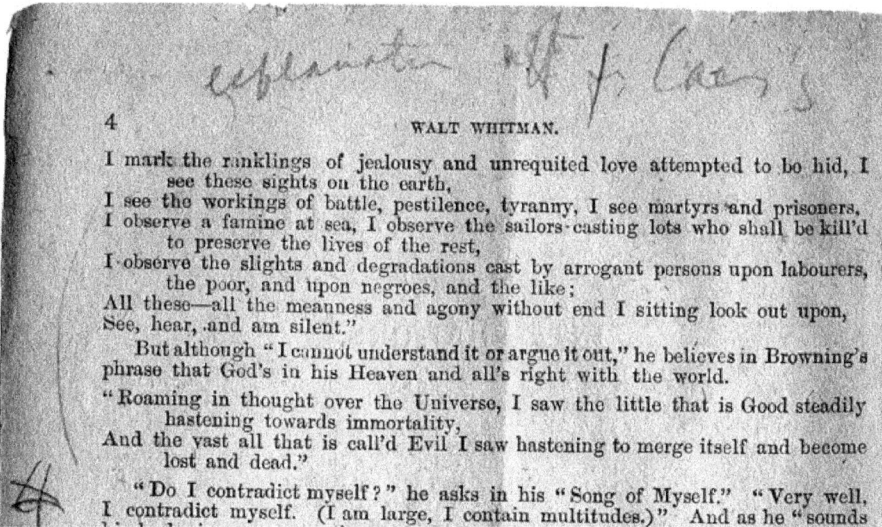

Detail of p. 4 of *Poems by Walt Whitman*.

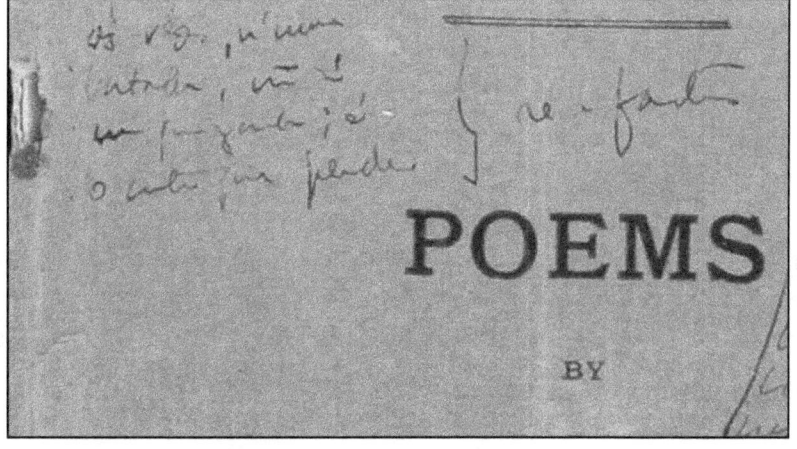

Cover of *Poems by Walt Whitman*.

---

[8] In section XVIII of "Song of Myself".

According to Mário Vítor Bastos, this annotation would be of considerable importance, because it would reassume the initially "battling" attitude of a Pessoa still adolescent and keen to compose beautiful verse in his confronting of a Whitman who had already got there, anticipating him by several decades (Bastos (b): 7). The closeness to the American poet would thus have followed an evolution similar to that expressed by Ezra Pound in his poem "A Pact", from 1908:

> I make a pact with you, Walt Whitman –
> I have detested you long enough.
> I come to you as a grown child
> Who has had a pig-headed father;
> I am old enough now to make friends.
> It was you that broke the new wood,
> Now it is a time for carving.
> We have one sap and one root –
> Let there be commerce between us. (Pound, 1975: 45)

We shall now move on to the second collection of Walt Whitman's poetry on the shelves of Pessoa's bookcases: *Leaves of Grass*. On this copy of 1909, Pessoa had written his own name and the date "16.5.1916" (Estibeira, 2008: 257). Such a practice was by no means new to Pessoa, who tended to sign and date the books in his possession.

The copy has annotations either in grey or lilac pencil, which suggest again that the Portuguese poet had done more than a single reading of the work, sometimes even correcting the punctuation. It is not difficult to itemize what had primarily touched Pessoa when he read *Leaves of Grass*. We may note, indeed, that the underlined elements add up to more than forty and, if we look at the marked passages, for example, in "Song of Myself", "Calamus", "Autumn Rivulets", "Whispers of Heavenly Death", "From Noon to Starry Night" and "Songs of Parting", we realize that they coincide with some of the main themes Pessoa inherited from Whitman: contact with rural nature, acceptance of reality as it is, universal complicity, abolition of the distinction between soul and body, subject and object, the self and others. We hear the echo of that sense of universal fraternity in the section of *Leaves of Grass* entitled "Calamus". There, Pessoa annotated several verses in the poems "To a Stranger" and "Salut au Monde!". This desire for solidarity and affection expressed by Whitman will come to be "incarnated" with surprising results in the Pessoa heteronym Álvaro de Campos who, in 1914, will show a certain frustration in exclaiming "Ah não ser eu toda a gente e toda a parte!" ["Ah not to be everyone and everywhere!"] (Pessoa 1993a: 144).

In his copy of *Leaves of Grass*, Pessoa also marked passages from "Song of Myself" in which the poet expressed the desire to assimilate all things; roots, mosses, fruits and animals. Pessoa had also marked verses contained in the poem "Years of the Modern" which referred to modern man, to his dreams and to the society in which he lived.

In "Sleepers", we discover an anticipation of Pessoan "outrar-se" ["othering"].

> I go from bedside to bedside, I sleep close with the other sleepers each in turn,
> I dream in my dream all the dreams of the other dreamers,
> And I become the other dreamers.

"Sleepers", in *Leaves of Grass*, p. 393.

> I am the actor, the actress, the voter, the politician,
> The emigrant and the exile, the criminal that stood in the box,
> He who has been famous and he who shall be famous after to-day,

"Sleepers", in *Leaves of Grass*, p. 393.

> I find I incorporate gneiss, coal, long-threaded moss, fruits, grains, esculent roots,
> And am stucco'd with quadrupeds and birds all over,
> And have distanced what is behind me for good reasons,
> But call anything back again when I desire it.

"Song of Myself", in *Leaves of Grass*, p. 67.

> TO A STRANGER
>
> PASSING stranger! you do not know how longingly I look upon you,
> You must be he I was seeking, or she I was seeking, (it comes to me as of a dream,)
> I have somewhere surely lived a life of joy with you,
> All is recall'd as we flit by each other, fluid, affectionate, chaste, matured,
> You grew up with me, were a boy with me or a girl with me,
> I ate with you and slept with you, <u>your body has become not yours only nor left my body mine only,</u>
> You give me the pleasure of your eyes, face, flesh, as we

"To a Stranger", in *Leaves of Grass*, p. 130.

> YEARS OF THE MODERN!
>
> YEARS of the modern! years of the unperform'd!
> Your horizon rises, I see it parting away for more august dramas,
> I see not America only, not only Liberty's nation but other nations preparing,
> I see tremendous entrances and exits, new combinations, the solidarity of races,
> I see that force advancing with irresistible power on the world's stage,
> (Have the old forces, the old wars, played their parts? are the acts suitable to them closed?)
> I see Freedom, completely arm'd and victorious and very haughty, with Law on one side and Peace on the other,
> A stupendous trio all issuing forth against the idea of caste;

"Years of the Modern!", in *Leaves of Grass*, p. 446.

We shall now consider the books *on* Whitman possessed by Pessoa and one in particular, *Walt Whitman's Anomaly*. The work in question is a study by Walter Rivers on some aspects of the life and literary works of the American writer (it included details pertaining to the presumed homosexuality of Whitman, the eponymous "anomaly") (Estibeira 2008: 263). The copy was signed by Pessoa himself and annotated in pencil with some regularity. Notes such as "!", "N.B.", "N.", "good", "g.", "curious", "excellent", "stupendous" and even the interjection "oh!" demonstrate the interest that the Portuguese poet had for this book.

> You Japanese man or woman! you liver in Madagascar, Ceylon, Sumatra, Borneo!
> All you continentals of Asia, Africa, Europe, Australia, indifferent of place!
> All you on the numberless islands of the archipelagoes of the sea!
> And you of centuries hence when you listen to me!
> And you each and everywhere whom I specify not, but include just the same!
> Health to you! good will to you all, from me and America sent!
>
> Each of us inevitable,
> Each of us limitless—each of us with his or her right upon the earth,
> Each of us allow'd the eternal purports of the earth,
> Each of us here as divinely as any is here.

"Salut au Monde", in *Leaves of Grass*, p. 146.

Chapter II
Whitman, writer of Pessoa

Turning to Pessoa, what'd he write about? Whitman,
(Lisbon, the sea etc.)...
Allen Ginsberg, "Salutations to Fernando Pessoa"

In the section of *Leaves of Grass* entitled "Inscriptions", Whitman launched an appeal to the future poets, a new choir of fledglings, so that they might give a definition and a justification to what he had been. In "Poets to come", we read:

Poets to come! orators, singers, musicians to come!
Not to-day is to justify me and answer what I am for,
But you, a new brood, native, athletic, continental, greater than before known,
Arouse! for you must justify me.

I myself but write one or two indicative words for the future,
I but advance a moment only to wheel and hurry back in the darkness.

I am a man who, sauntering along without fully stopping, turns a casual look upon you
and then averts his face,
Leaving it to you to prove and define it,
Expecting the main things from you.

Pessoa, who in his copy of *Leaves of Grass* had underlined the last verse, was undoubtedly one of the first of that new breed of poets to respond to the call of the American writer. To do so, he availed himself of the unbridled Álvaro de Campos and the apparently *naïf* Alberto Caeiro.

We shall focus firstly on Álvaro de Campos, the heteronym "cosmopolite par formation et hystérique par constitution" ["cosmopolite by training and hysterical by constitution"] (Perrone-Moisés 2014: 114). By his own account, we know that he was born in 1890 (two years before the death of Walt Whitman) in Portugal, and that he graduated from the University of Glasgow in naval engineering. In 1914, he signed "Ode Triunfal", published a year later in the first number of the journal *Orpheu*, emblematic outlet for the first Portuguese Modernism. Campos founded, then, *sensacionismo* [sensationism], a movement whose slogan was, in the poem "A Passagem das Horas" ["The Passing of Hours"], "Sentir tudo de todas as maneiras" ["Feel everything in every way"]. Antonio Tabucchi defined the poetry of the avant-garde Pessoan heteronym as something that might turn futurist, applying it to the love for the machine age and for the modern, the pantheism and the pluralism of the loved and hated Whitman (Tabucchi and Lancastre 2007: 50).

The name of Álvaro de Campos has often been associated with the futurist movement. However, when it comes to attaching labels, we always prefer to adopt a little caution. Re-adapting a claim made by Leyla Perrone-Moisés, we shall say that "[Campos] n'est pas futuriste, mais futurible" ["Campos is not futurist, but futurable"] (Perrone-Moisés 2014: 119). Indeed, even though he appears to be a faithful follower of Marinetti, we believe that his closest work to Futurism is limited to but a few texts, perhaps the most notable of them being "Ode Triunfal", "Ode Marítima" ["Maritime Ode"] (1914), "Saudação a Walt Whitman" ["Salutation to Walt Whitman"] (1915) and "Ultimatum" (1917). It is primarily in these works that Campos uses onomatopoeia and innumerable typographical devices to sing the praise of modern life, the crowd, speed, electricity and the machine. These same works are, however, also indebted to the poetry of Whitman.

We may begin by analyzing what, from the title alone, seems to be the most immediate tribute to the singer of *Leaves of Grass*, "Saudação a Walt Whitman". Dated 11 June 1915, this ode, of which there are only fragments, was never finished and remained unpublished until after the death of Fernando Pessoa. The title recalls that of the poem "Salut au Monde!", in which Whitman addressed the whole world. Differently, Campos decided to pay homage to just one man. Turning to Whitman, Álvaro de Campos not only drew on Whitman-like rhythms but also appropriated and mimicked the prosody, the rhetoric, the imagery, the themes and the attitudes of Whitman (Santos 2003: 66). Besides the free verse and the torrential flow of Whitman-style syntax, we find enumerations, repetitions, juxtapositions and syncopations. There is the introduction of foreign words and the recourse to a feverish punctuation. We are witness to explosions of oxymorons accompanied by strong sexual imagery. In the Campos composition, there are, among other things, a frantic use of apostrophe, the collision of time and space, the bold arrogance of the verse and the wild celebration of an unusual range of objects. There are, in short, an acute awareness of modernity and progress, pride in confronting conventional ideas and emotions, a marveling at liberty and democracy ("Libertad! Democracy!"), everything together with a shiver at the discovery of the body. Distinguishable, above all, is the solidarity, the empathy, the approval or, as Campos has it, the "contiguity" of Whitman.[9]

"Saudação a Walt Whitman" is notably long, therefore we shall take into consideration only those passages that might be deemed crucial to our argument here. Thus, for instance, the first verses of the section:

Portugal-Infinito, onze de Junho de mil novecentos e quinze...
Hé-lá-á-á-á-á-á-á!
De aqui, de Portugal, todas as épocas no meu cérebro,
Saúdo-te, Walt, saúdo-te, meu irmão em Universo...

[Portugal-Infinite, eleven June nineteen fifteen...
Hé-lá-á-á-á-á-á-á!
From here, from Portugal, all eras in my brain,
I salute you, Walt, I salute you, my Universal brother...]

The poem begins with the typical opening of a commercial letter Pessoa was used to writing that placed the poet in space and time: "Portugal-Infinito" (as if it were "Lisbon, Portugal" or "Camden, New York"), "1915". The rest ensues

---

[9] A line from "Saudação a Walt Whitman" is: "Quero a contiguidade penetrada e material dos objectos!" ["I want the penetrated and material contiguity of objects"].

following the initial apostrophe typical of the ode. In this case, the apostrophe is a fractious yell (almost parodying the "barbaric yawp"). In fact, the whole poem may be considered one long apostrophe that flows in an unmistakable dialogical and anaphoric Whitman-like structure. The effect is sustained by the continuous use of the vocative. The North-American writer is saluted as a hot concubine of a dispersed Universe, a great pederast who rubs up against the diversity of things, a great "epidermic democratic", contiguous with everything in body and soul, Milton-Shelley of the horizon of future Electricity, *souteneur* of the whole Universe, prostitute of all solar systems, God's faggot. The verses of Campos become the stage on which the two poets join in solidarity as brothers of the Universe. Campos, indeed, requests the Bard not to be unworthy of him, but rather to consider him "one of [his] own". He confesses, further, to understanding and loving Whitman exactly as Whitman has understood and loved him, despite the fact that the two never knew each other personally:

> Sei que me conheceste, que me contemplaste e me explicaste,
> Sei que é isso que eu sou, quer em Brooklyn Ferry dez anos antes de eu nascer,
> Quer pela rua do Ouro acima pensando em tudo que não é a rua do Ouro,
> E conforme tu sentiste tudo, sinto tudo, e cá estamos de mãos dadas,
> De mãos dadas, Walt, de mãos dadas, dançando o universo na alma.
>
> [I know that you knew me, that you contemplated and explained me,
> I know that that's what I am, whether on the Brooklyn Ferry ten years before I was born,
> Or in the Rua do Ouro, thinking about everything that is not the Rua do Ouro,
> And just as you felt everything, I feel everything, and here we are holding hands,
> Holding hands, Walt, holding hands, the Universe dancing in our souls.]

In our view, this is a particularly noteworthy passage, in the first place because of the affirmation made by Campos: "I know that you knew me, that you contemplated and explained me". It would appear that, here, Pessoa-

Campos had in mind the previously quoted Whitman poem, "Poets to Come". The Portuguese writer inverted Whitman's appeal: whilst in the American text the poet casts a casual glance and then looks away and asks that it be the new generation of poets that "define him", in the Campos ode the subject feels observed and defined by Whitman.

Yet, there is also a further noteworthy element that is the simultaneous presence of the "Brooklyn Ferry" and of the "Rua do Ouro". The Brooklyn Ferry is the synthesis of America seen through the eyes of Pessoa-Campos: "Crossing Brooklyn Ferry" is the title of a poem in *Leaves of Grass*, which Pessoa, on his copy, had several times underlined. The Rua do Ouro is, rather, one of the most central streets in Lisbon. The co-existence of the two in Campos's ode points to the desire of the Portuguese writer to resituate the lyrical axis away from the United States to Portugal.

We would also emphasize the lines "E conforme tu sentiste tudo, sinto tudo, e cá estamos de mãos dadas/ De mãos dadas, Walt, de mãos dadas, dançando o universo na alma", because, besides best reassuming the spirit of *sensacionismo*, they seem to be a reply to the sequence "A Leaf for Hand in Hand" in the section entitled "Calamus" of *Leaves of Grass*. Here, Whitman calls on all, young and old, boatmen and machine workers from all the parts of the Mississippi, exclaiming, "I wish to infuse myself among you till I see it common for you to walk hand in hand!". The insistence on the phrase "de mãos dadas" in the composition of Campos is also certainly an echo of the first verse of "Salut au Monde!", which is cited, in the emphatic "O take my hand Walt Whitman!".

Proceeding with "Saudação a Walt Whitman", we read:

Olha pra mim: tu sabes que eu, Álvaro de Campos, engenheiro,
Poeta sensacionista,
Não sou teu discípulo, não sou teu amigo, não sou teu cantor,
Tu sabes que eu sou Tu e estás contente com isso!

[Look at me: you know that I, Álvaro de Campos, engineer,
Sensationist poet,
Am not your disciple, am not your friend, am not your singer,
You know that I am You and you are content with that!]

This is only one of so many exhortations that recur in the text (such as, for example, "Dança comigo, Walt" ["Dance with me, Walt"], "Salta comigo" ["Jump with me"], "Cai comigo" ["Fall with me"], "Esbarra comigo tonto nas paredes" ["Bang the walls crazily with me"], "Parte-te e esfrangalha-te comigo" ["Divide yourself and fragment yourself with me"]). In this case, Campos wants Whitman to look at him and recognize that the heteronym is not just his disciple or his friend: Campos *is* Whitman.

Therefore, after a first section in which the American poet is defined, and after a second part in which Campos takes stock of who he is, there is a third moment in the ode which bears witness to Campos's identification with Whitman. Underlining the curious manner in which the poet describes himself ("eu, Álvaro de Campos, engenheiro,/ Poeta sensacionista") is perhaps an adaptation of section XXIV of "Song of Myself", in which Whitman characterizes himself as "Walt Whitman, a kosmos, of Manhattan the son".

We concede that whoever examines Pessoa's copy of *Leaves of Grass* can only guess at the emotion with which the young Portuguese writer approached the poetry of Whitman. There is, however, a sense of discovery pervading the annotations left in the margins of the texts – the feeling of a sudden awakening. It is a feeling similar to the one of which Campos speaks in the following passage of "Saudação a Walt Whitman":

Nunca posso ler os teus versos a fio... Há ali sentir de mais...
Atravesso os teus versos como a uma multidão aos encontrões a mim,
E cheira-me a suor, a óleos, a actividade humana e mecânica
Nos teus versos, a certa altura não sei se leio ou se vivo,
Não sei se o meu lugar real é no mundo ou nos teus versos...

[I can never read your verses all at once... There is too much feeling in them...
I traverse your verse as if it were a crowd rushing at me,
And it smells to me of sweat, of oils, of human and mechanical activity
In your verse, at times, I know not whether I am reading or living,
I know not whether my real place is in the world or in your verse...]

Such is the violent impact of Whitman on Pessoa-Campos. The writer openly confesses that he cannot read the verses of the American Bard at one go, because of the excess of sensations that they contain. Whitman's lines, for the Portuguese poet, are like an onrushing crowd that overwhelms him, smelling of oil and sweat. The immediacy with which Whitman shows himself in his own poetry is without doubt either seductive or menacing for Campos, who fears being suffocated by the intensity of confused sentiments that the Long Island poet evokes.

Proceeding with the ode, Campos admits that he does not know whether his feet are on the ground or whether his head is upside down, hanging from the roof of the "inaccessible intensity" of Walt. The image of the poet upside down will appear, too, in another composition by Pessoa's heteronym, "A Passagem das Horas" (1916): here, Campos will find himself "de cabeça para baixo" ["with his head down"] at the centre of his own self-consciousness.[10] In the episode "I – A Múmia" ["I – A mummy"] from "Episódios" (1917), Pessoa himself will write, again:

> Floresceu às avessas
> Meu ócio sem-nexo
>
> [My linkless loafing
> Bloomed inside-out]

And a little further on:

> E o deserto está agora
> Virado para baixo.
>
> [And the desert now
> Turned upside down]

In a poem from 1914, Bernardo Soares wrote "Árvores longínquas que

---

[10] "Eu de cabeça pra baixo no centro da minha consciência de mim..." in "A Passagem das Horas".

esperam por mim desde Deus" ["Distant trees that from God await me"],[11] and Campos, one year later, in "Saudação a Walt Whitman", writes: "olha pra mim, de aí desde Deus vês-me ao contrário" ["look at me, from there from God you see me back to front"]. It is our view that the recurrence of the figure of the poet the wrong way round is not accidental and, rather, may be a reminder of Odin. In the Nordic tradition, this divinity is known under eighty-four different names, each of which reflects a characteristic specific to its bearer. He is commonly associated with wisdom and poetic inspiration. In order to obtain wisdom, it is said that he had given an eye to the fountain of the giant Mímir. In this way, while one eye remained to observe the world of external reality, the other turned inwards to explore the infinite inner worlds. Odin knows the secrets of the runes, the letters that, cut in wood, on stone, on the blades of swords, on the tongues of poets, on the hooves of horses, are the very origin of all knowledge and all power. In order to learn the art of the runes, and of divination, in "Hávamal" (the second poem of the *Poetic Edda*) it is told that Odin was held against a tree, head upside down, for nine days and nights. The figure of the Hanged Man on the twelfth Major Arcana would itself be inspired by this Nordic divinity and it is for this reason that, in the traditional representation, the left eye of the Hanged Man is closed, while the right eye attentively observes the rune stone at the foot of the ash tree. In our reading, Pessoa, given his esoteric interests, is able to reference the Tarot cards. In the text "A Hora do Diabo" ["The Hour of the Devil"], for example, there is an explicit mention of the eighteenth Arcanum, the one representing the Moon.

Pessoa had underlined in his copy of *Leaves of Grass* these two lines from "Song of Myself":

Unscrew the locks from the doors!
Unscrew the doors themselves from their jambs!

They can be juxtaposed with the following passage from "Saudação a Walt Whitman":

---

[11] It is a poem whose first line is: "Como quem, roçando um arco às vezes" ["Like someone stroking a bow at times"] (Pessoa 1982: 269).

Abram-me todas as portas!
Por força que hei-de passar!
Minha senha? Walt Whitman!
Mas não dou senha nenhuma...
Passo sem explicações...
Se for preciso meto dentro as portas...

[Open all the doors for me!
Perforce I shall have to pass through!
My password? Walt Whitman!
But I'm giving no password...
I pass through without explanations...
If necessary, I'll break down the doors...]

Whitman ordered an unlocking of the doors, removal of doors from their hinges. Campos wants all doors to be open to him: he must perforce pass through and his password is "Walt Whitman". He demands to pass through without offering explanations to anyone and, if necessary, he is even prepared to batter down any obstacles in his way. Álvaro de Campos, however "franzinho e civilizado" ["weak and civilized"], would indeed beat down all doors, because he feels like "um universo pensante de carne e osso" ["a thinking universe of flesh and bone"] who wants to pass through, to transcend – and, when he aspires so to do, he is God! This is a Campos who, explicitly empowered by the named precursor, thus spurs on the very horse which he bestrides... the self:

Sinto as esporas, sou o próprio cavalo em que monto,
Porque eu, por minha vontade de me consubstanciar com Deus,
Posso ser tudo, ou posso ser nada, ou qualquer coisa,
Conforme me der na gana... Ninguém tem nada com isso...

[I feel the spurs, I am the very horse that I mount,
Because I, through my will to be consubstantial with God,
Can be all, or nothing, or anything,
Whatever I want... No one has anything to do with that.]

These last two verses in particular recall a poem of Whitman that Pessoa had countersigned and at which we have already hinted. They are the verses 84-85 of "Crossing Brooklyn Ferry", where we read:

> The same old role, the role that is what we make it, as great as we like,
> Or as small as we like, or both great and small.

> Play'd the part that still looks back on the actor or actress,
> The same old role, the role that is what we make it, as great as we like,
> Or as small as we like, or both great and small.
>
> 7
>
> Closer yet I approach you,
> What thought you have of me now, I had as much of you—
> I laid in my stores in advance,
> I consider'd long and seriously of you before you were born.

"Crossing Brooklyn Ferry", in *Leaves of Grass*, p. 162.

Turning again to the ode by Campos, there is another step that expresses the need of the poet to unhinge the doors in order to impose upon the reader his own individuality as an all-inclusive Universe.

> Abram-me todas as janelas!
> Arranquem-me todas as portas!
> Puxem a casa toda para cima de mim!
> Quero viver em liberdade no ar,
> Quero ter gestos fora do meu corpo,
> Quero correr como a chuva pelas paredes abaixo,
> Quero ser pisado nas estradas largas como as pedras,
> Quero ir, como as coisas pesadas, para o fundo dos mares,
> Com uma voluptuosidade que já está longe de mim!
>
> [Open to me all the windows!
> Wrench off for me all the doors!

Pull down the whole house on top of me!
I want to live at liberty in the air,
I want to gesture beyond my body,
I want to run like rain down the walls,
I want to be trodden on broad roads like stones,
I want to go, as do heavy things, down to the bottom of the sea,
With a voluptuousness that is still far from me!]

Campos demands that every window be open to him and that all doors be removed (even that the whole house be carried off), because he wants to be free, to stream like the rain over walls, to be as trodden as the paving stones on the roads. It is not accidentally that the poet turns to Whitman as if he were "Porta p'ra tudo!/ Ponte p'ra tudo!/ Estrada p'ra tudo!" ["Door to everything!/ Bridge to everything!/ Road to everything!"], and as if he were the last "unhinger". In order to dance with Walt the "raiva abstracta do corpo fazendo maelstroms na alma" ["abstract fury of body making maelstroms in the soul"], Campos rejects the very existence of door locks and of fastened chests:

Não quero fechos nas portas!
Não quero fechaduras nos cofres!
Quero intercalar-me, imiscuir-me, ser levado...

[I don't want closed doors!
I don't want locked chests!
I want to intercalate me, to mix me, to be carried away...]

At this point, let us make a brief reference, in passing, to Gaston Bachelard. He points out that the house encloses a *corpus* of images that give man means to achieve, or illusions of, stability. The house is 1) imagined as being vertical, upright; and 2) imagined as a concentrated entity. The verticality is assured by the polarity attic/basement: between the two exists the same strong opposition as between rational and irrational. For the poet, the roof signifies freedom and the possibility of ascending to the clouds. On the contrary, the cellar is the dark self of the house, the element that stands alongside the underground powers. In the attic, once night is gone, up comes the clarity of the day. The basement, on the contrary, remains ever dark.

According to Carlos D'Alge, in his "Saudação a Walt Whitman" Álvaro de Campos was beginning his emergence towards the attic in order to see the light and to break out of the nightmare of darkness (whence the exclamation "Abram-me todas as janelas!") (D'Alge 1989: 80). D'Alge draws our attention further to Campos's rejection of locks. A locked chest holds secrets and can betoken promises. Arthur Rimbaud, in "Les Étrennes des Orphelins" ["The Orphans' Christmas Box"], celebrated thus the sleeping mysteries of an antique wardrobe that had no keys:

- L'armoire était sans clefs !... sans clefs, la grande armoire !
On regardait souvent sa porte brune et noire...
Sans clefs !... c'était étrange !... on rêvait bien des fois
Aux mystères dormant entre ses flancs de bois,
Et l'on croyait ouïr, au fond de la serrure
Béante, un bruit lointain, vague et joyeux murmure...

[The wardrobe had no keys!... no keys, the great wardrobe!
We often looked upon its brown and black door...
No keys!... how strange!... We dreamed oft times
Of mysteries dormant within its wooden sides,
And we thought we heard, from deep inside its gaping lock,
A distant noise, a vague and joyous whisper...]

The coffer, the wardrobe and the door constitute closed systems; but for the new man of the twentieth century each lock is an invitation to a safebreaker. Álvaro de Campos is, indeed, the safebreaker who refuses to find himself confronted by an inviolable space.

Returning to the ode, when the subject appears to have reached the high point of emotive release, the flow of the poem is strangely interrupted:

Arre! Vamos lá pra frente!
[...]

(Deixa-me tirar a gravata e desabotoar o colarinho.
Não se pode ter muita energia com a civilização à roda do pescoço...)
Agora, sim, partamos, vá lá pra frente.

[Gee up! Let's move on!
[...]
(Let me take off my tie and unbutton my collar.
There can't be much energy with civilization hanging round my neck...)
Now, yes, let's leave, let's move on.]

Campos's gesture is undoubtedly indebted to Ezra Pound who, in his essay of 1909, "What I feel about Walt Whitman", wrote:

Mentally I am a Walt Whitman who has learned to wear a collar and a dress shirt (although at times inimical to both).

Irene Ramalho de Sousa Santos observes that at a fifth from the end of "Saudação a Walt Whitman", an alien voice, as if it were the indication of a director, says (in English and in italics in the original): "He calls Walt". If "He" is Álvaro de Campos, then the scene director must be Fernando Pessoa. From the privileged point of view of the director (the infinite, the Universe), Campos (born in 1890) and Whitman (who died in 1892) are "brothers". Side by side, "dançando o universo na alma", the two poets are but one, identical. They are like the heteronyms, close but not equal. As Ramalho, the author of *Atlantic Poets*, clarifies:

Rather than brothers, they are other(s). (Santos 2003: 71)

At the end of the ode, we read:

Agora que estou quase na morte e vejo tudo já claro,
Grande Libertador, volto submisso a ti.

[Now that I am nearly in death and see all so clearly,
Great Liberator, I turn submissively to you.]

Here, Campos's subject, overcome with fatigue and on the point of dying, turns submissively to a Whitman perceived as the Great Liberator. It might well be asked why there is such docility after the vitalistic explosions of the preceding verses. It would appear that, at the close, the Portuguese poet admits to himself that he is not at Whitman's level. Despite the cockiness with which he had affirmed his own identity ("Eu, Álvaro de Campos, [...]/ eu sou Tu"), the heteronym ends up stating the impossibility of being "other". Thus, a composition that was apparently a simply homage to the author of *Leaves of Grass* turns out to be a poem on diversity. The tones soften eventually in the final verses of the ode:

> Sem dúvida teve um fim a minha personalidade.
> Sem dúvida porque se exprimiu, quis dizer qualquer coisa
> Mas hoje, olhando pra trás, só uma ânsia me fica –
> Não ter tido a tua calma superior a ti-próprio,
> A tua libertação consteladada de Noite Infinita.
>
> Não tive talvez missão alguma na terra.
>
> [Without doubt, there was an end to my personality.
> Without doubt, because it was expressed, it meant something
> But today, looking back, only one worry stays with me –
> Not to have had your calm superior to yourself,
> Your constellated liberty of Infinite Night.
>
> I had perhaps no mission on earth.]

At the end of "Saudação a Walt Whitman", as at the end of "Ode Triunfal" and "Ode Marítima", the attitude of Campos is that of someone who has been defeated. In this case, Campos, looking into himself, realizes that he has never possessed that "calma superior" typical of Whitman. Rather, he suspects he has never had any mission to fulfil on earth.

Apropos of the "superior calm" of the North-American poet, Richard Zenith's position is of some interest. In his essay, "Pessoa and Walt Whitman Revisited", Zenith maintains that "Saudação a Walt Whitman" does not sound like any poetry of the Long Island writer. It does make several allusions to Whitman's poetry, counter some of his topics, make use of similar syntactical structures, and the style of the verse would recall that of Whitman, but the tone is different and the whole is expressed at a different speed, more rapid than that of the American poet (Zenith 2013: 37). Campos, unlike Whitman, is restless, frenetic, at times hysterical. Whitman always keeps a "calma superior" – with the exception of his "barbaric yawp". Not to be excluded, in our view, is the fact that Campos appropriates the rowdy barbaric yawp of Whitman with both a celebratory and a parodic intent. It is possible, therefore, to reconsider the use of the apostrophe in Campos's text.

One stimulating reading of "Saudação a Walt Whitman" is that of Susan Margaret Brown: "I had originally wanted to say that it is the characteristic dialogue of self and soul in both Whitman and Pessoa that provides the central *hinge* between the two poets" (Brown 1988: 35). However, because of a typographical mistake, what should have read "central *hinge*" became "central *binge*". When, years later, Brown corrected the error, she also observed how appropriate, in fact, the play on words had been. If it were possible to speak about "word binge" or "language binge", Walt Whitman and Álvaro de Campos would certainly be egregious examples of such verbal intoxication. Thinking of just "Song of Myself", "Saudação a Walt Whitman", "Ode Triunfal" and "A Passagem das Horas", we find texts in which the dominant note is verbal energy, the force of words that aim at wrapping up everything, devouring the whole Universe. Whitman himself boasts, in section XXV of "Song of Myself", "My voice goes after what my eyes cannot reach,/ With the twirl of my tongue I encompass worlds and volumes of worlds". According to Brown, what links the two poets is captured here. In both, there is the strong desire to free language, to let it go, drunk on its own power. Campos and Whitman strive to let the word shatter all chains, distending and expanding to cover the Universe of the page. In order to transgress the limits of language, some distinguished liberators are called for. It is not accidentally that Campos addresses his "Universal brother" as "Grande Libertador".

A further great liberation, for which Whitman might be a model, the sexual one, emerges in more sequences of "Saudação a Walt Whitman". The American writer is saluted as a "Grande Pederasta" ["Great Pederast"] who appears to be "sexualizado pelas pedras, pelas árvores, pelas pessoas, pelas profissões" ["sexualized by stones, by trees, by people, by professions"]. This is not the moment to discuss the matter in detail but, as we shall illustrate, Pessoa was preoccupied by his own "sexual inversion" and by the "feminine temperament" which he was convinced he had. In a letter to João Gaspar Simões of 18 November 1930, he confessed to having the "obscene" English poems and the work of homoerotic taste, "Antinous", for the purpose of expelling the "obscenity" from his system and feeling himself ready for the "superior mental processes" to which he believed himself predestined. Indubitably, a certain importance can be derived from the fact that "Saudação a Walt Whitman" is not signed by Pessoa himself, but by a heteronym. Galloping alongside Walt, Campos (and Pessoa through him) would thus have gained the freedom of being anything.

More than a century after the writing of "Salut au Monde!", and seventy years after that of "Saudação a Walt Whitman", Allen Ginsberg published a cheeky and sarcastic parody, "Salutations to Fernando Pessoa". We here reproduce Ginsberg's opening lines:

Everytime I read Pessoa I think
I'm better than he is I do the same thing
more extravagantly – he's only from Portugal,
I'm American greatest Country in the world

At the outset of this chapter on Pessoa as reader/interpreter of Whitman, we cited several texts by Álvaro de Campos – the ones that are generally considered "futurist" – that we consider to be indebted to the Whitman experience. Among these, we included, in addition to "Saudação a Walt Whitman", "Ode Triunfal" and "Ode Marítima". Let us begin by addressing the first of them, which Eduardo Lourenço defined as "hiperbólico hossana [...] à explosiva e premente novidade do mundo e sobretudo aos seus aspectos mais agressiva e perturbadoramente modernos" ["hyperbolic hosanna to the exploding and pressing newness of the world and, above all, to his most aggressively and perturbingly modern aspects"] (Lourenço 1973: 76). According to Ramalho, there are only a few poems in the Western tradition that, like "Ode Triunfal", confront so directly the poetical, political and sexual contradictions of modernity (Santos 2003: 162). In "Ode Triunfal", Campos advances towards the reader apparently without any mask, following the rhythm and the formally joyous musicality of Walt Whitman. The ode opens thus:

> À dolorosa luz das grandes lâmpadas eléctricas da fábrica
> Tenho febre e escrevo,
> Escrevo rangendo os dentes, fera para a beleza disto,
> Para a beleza disto totalmente desconhecida dos antigos.
>
> [In the painful light of the great electric factory lamps
> I feverishly write,
> I write grinding my teeth, wild at the beauty of all this,
> For the beauty of all this unknown to the ancients.]

In the painful light of the factory lamps, the poet feverishly writes – and he does it grinding his teeth, as if he were a beast in front of the beauty of whatever surrounds it, a beauty completely unknown to the ancients. Campos pursues a frenetic eulogy to machines, wheels, motors, transmission belts and pistons – in substance, to the "eternal r-r-r-r-r-r" and the "Z-z-z-z-z-z-z-z-z-z-z". The impetus and the arrogance of Campos's verses call to mind "A Song of Joys", a poem contained in the "Calamus" section of *Leaves of Grass*:

> It is not enough to have this globe or a certain time,
> I will have thousands of globes and all time.
> O the engineer's joys! to go with a locomotive!
> To hear the hiss of steam, the merry shriek, the steam-whistle, the laughing locomotive!
> To push with resistless way and speed off in the distance.

Here Whitman (anticipating from a great distance futurist provocations) was not content with a single planet and a determined time. His longing for the infinite would be taken up by Marinetti who, in "Manifesto del Futurismo" of 1909, would declare: "Il Tempo e lo Spazio morirono ieri. Noi viviamo già nell'assoluto, poiché abbiamo già creata l'eterna velocità onnipresente" ["Time and Space died yesterday. We live already in the absolute, since we have already created the eternal omnipresent speed"].

In the poem "A Song of Joys", towards the end, we read:

O to have life henceforth a poem of new joys!
To dance, clap hands, exult, shout, skip, leap, roll on, float on!
To be a sailor of the world bound for all ports,
A ship itself, (see indeed these sails I spread to the sun and air,)
A swift and swelling ship full of rich words, full of joys.

Some decades on, in "Ode Triunfal", we find:

Mas, ah, outra vez a raiva mecânica constante!
Outra vez a obsessão movimentada dos ómnibus.
E outra vez a fúria de estar indo ao mesmo tempo dentro de todos os comboios
De todas as partes do mundo,
De estar dizendo adeus de bordo de todos os navios,
Que a estas horas estão levantando ferro ou afastando-se das docas.

[But, oh, again the constant mechanical rage!
Again the agitated obsession of the omnibuses.
And once again the fury of traveling at the same time in every train
In every part of the world,
Of saying farewell from the deck of every ship,
Which at this moment is weighing anchor or drawing away from the docks.]

Campos expresses in this passage the desire of travelling at the same time in every train towards every part of the world and of greeting from all the ships that are setting sail. We share Lourenço's opinion that this ode, obviously Whitman-like in its momentum, in its choice of images and in its mode of piling them up, may be even more Whitmanish in the exaltation of eroticism that structures it. The verse that Mário de Sá-Carneiro, friend and modernist colleague of Pessoa, most admired in "Ode Triunfal" had been bracketed by Campos and quoted: "(Ah, como eu desejaria ser o *souteneur* disto tudo!)" ["(Ah, how I would like to be the *souteneur* of all this!)"]. We recall that, in "Saudação a Walt Whitman", the poet addressed Whitman by calling him "*Souteneur* de todo o Universo".

Our interest does not focus on the sexuality of poets, rather on the way in which their poetry is sexualized. Ramalho refers to "intersexuality" to define the androgynous assimilation, on the part of the poet, of an ancient muse within the masculine self proper. This incorporation would be none other than the expression of feminine desire of the artist (Santos 2003: 176). According to the author of *Atlantic Poets*, no one had more clamorously celebrated intersexual identity prior to the appearance of Álvaro de Campos, the engineer with the insatiable ambition of wanting to feel everything in every possible manner. Such a sensationist longing refers, as well, to the most extreme sexual experiences. Let us skim these avid and passionate lines from "Ode Triunfal":

Poder ao menos penetrar-me fisicamente de tudo isto,
Rasgar-me todo, abrir-me completamente, tornar-me passento
A todos os perfumes de óleos e calores e carvões
Desta flora estupenda, negra, artificial e insaciável!

[If at least I could penetrate myself physically with all this,
Tear myself wholly apart, open myself completely, become pervious
To all the perfumes from the oils and hot coals
Of this stupendous, black, artificial and insatiable flora!]

James E. Miller has also coined a word that might embrace the erotic and sexual dimension in its totality: "omnisexuality". The said term would point to "all sexual feeling of all conceivable kind" (Alves and Cid 1999: 29) and would be typically Whitman-like, though it is possible to trace its presence in lines from Campos, too:

Como eu vos amo a todos, a todos, a todos,
Como eu vos amo de todas as maneiras,

Com os olhos e com os ouvidos e com o olfacto
E com o tacto (o que palpar-vos representa para mim!)
E com a inteligência como uma antena que fazeis vibrar!
Ah, como todos os meus sentidos têm cio de vós!

[How I love all of you, all of you, all of you,
How I love you in every possible way,
With my eyes and with my ears and with my smell
And with my touch (what touching you is for me!)
And with my intelligence like an antenna that you make vibrate!
Ah, how all my senses lust for you!]

On other occasions, the Pessoan heteronym declares what is conveyed by the Portuguese word "cio", that is, the strong sexual appetite, "the hots", the animal desire to be conjoined with anyone and with anything:

Amo-vos a todos, a tudo, como uma fera.
Amo-vos carnivoramente,
Pervertidamente e enroscando a minha vista
Em vós, ó coisas grandes, banais, úteis, inúteis,
Ó coisas todas modernas,
Ó minhas contemporâneas, forma actual e próxima
Do sistema imediato do Universo!
Nova Revelação metálica e dinâmica de Deus!

[I love you all, and everything, like a wild beast.
I love you carnivorously,
Pervertedly and twisting my sight
Into you, oh great, banal, useful, useless things,
Oh all modern things,
Oh my contemporary, present and nearby things
Of the immediate system of the Universe!
New metallic and dynamic Revelation of God!]

The poet, wrapping with his gaze all the things of modernity, falls in love with them in the flesh and perversely. The senses of Campos are galvanized before the symbols of the Modern that the Pessoan heteronym wants to possess as if possessing a beautiful woman we do not love, but we meet casually and find extremely fascinating:

Ó fábricas, ó laboratórios, ó music-halls, ó Luna-Parks,
Ó couraçados, ó pontes, ó docas flutuantes –
Na minha mente turbulenta e encandescida
Possuo-vos como a uma mulher bela,
Completamente vos possuo como a uma mulher bela que não se ama,
Que se encontra casualmente e se acha interessantíssima.

[Oh factories, oh laboratories, oh music-halls, oh Luna-Parks,
Oh battleships, oh bridges, oh floating docks –
In my turbulent and incandescent mind
I possess you as a beautiful woman,
I possess you completely like a beautiful woman who isn't loved,
Who's casually encountered and is absolutely interesting.]

Whitman already, in his "Song of Myself", had hugged, and from that very moment possessed, all the men, the women, the slaves, the weak and the dying that he had encountered along the way:

I have embraced you, and henceforth possess you to myself,
And when you rise in the morning you will find what I tell you is so.

Still on the theme of possession, Álvaro de Campos shall write in "A Passagem das Horas":

Todos são a minha amante predilecta pelo menos um momento na vida.

[All are my favourite lover at least for one moment in life.]

He will add, further, "Só amando os homens, as acções, a banalidade dos trabalhos,/ Só assim – ai de mim! – só assim se pode viver" ["Only loving men, actions, the banality of work,/ Only thus – oh dear – only like that can one live"].

In "Ode Triunfal", half way through, Campos affirms that he could die knocked down by a car, with the delicious sentiment of a possessed woman who abandons herself. He exhorts, therefore, that they throw him into furnaces, throw him under trains and strike him on ships – he thus defines masochism through machinisms.

> Espanquem-me a bordo de navios!
> Masoquismo através de maquinismos!
> Sadismo de não sei quê moderno e eu e barulho!
>
> [Let them spank me aboard ships!
> Masochism through machinisms!
> Sadism of I don't know what, modern, me and din!]

More than denying the exaltation of Marinetti's "azione aggressiva" ["aggressive action"], these lines of Campos evoke well the erotically passive character that pervades the ode. The erotic passivity of Álvaro de Campos is a theme we shall address more fully in the final chapter. Meanwhile, it is instructive to note how this voluntary submission finds expression at other points of "Ode Triunfal".

Voyeurism can be an example of passivity and there is a moment in which Campos exclaims that for him seeing is "uma perversão sexual!" ["a sexual perversion"]. At another point, the poet appeals to trams, funiculars and metros so that they rub against him "até ao espasmo" ["until spasm"]. In the final verses of the ode, the writer is hooked to every train, lifted on every dock and made to rotate in the propellers of every ship – the realization and culmination of the machine-borne sado-masochism of modernity.

We have been made aware, thanks to a succession of studies by Jacinto do Prado Coelho, José Augusto Seabra and Eduardo Lourenço, that the legitimate meaning of "Ode Triunfal" does not reside in the beauty of machines but rather in the sensations these same machines provoke. Álvaro de Campos is truly the singer of progress and of speed – concrete realities that we cannot ignore – but, as Lourenço proposes, perhaps it would be more correct to call him a "des-cantor" ["dis-chanter"], if the term existed (Lourenço 1973: 96). The intensely negative nature of the approaching of the Modern, marked by the triumph of technics, is announced without hesitation at the very same opening of the text: it is at the *painful* light of the electric lamps of the factory that the poet has a fever and writes. Ramalho is of the view that Campos's futurist vision is, in fact, futureless – it is rather an incessant return to the time and space of an atemporal "Natureza tropical" ["Tropical nature"]: "Rather than a celebration of progress, 'Ode Triunfal' is a powerful demystification of its ideology" (Santos 2003: 184).

In reality, what theoretically should be the celebration of modern technology is nothing but an avant-gardiste soap bubble, which explodes a little melancholically. The "modernolatry" alternates continually with a sort of archaic nostalgia for the past, clearly a legacy of Decadentism. As a result, what emerges from Campos's ode, all things considered, is a "futurism" declined *à la portugaise* that searches in future man for an escape or liberation from a present in which, probably, the man of the moment felt uneasy.

"Ode Marítima" was published for the first time in 1915, in the second number of the journal *Orpheu*. Worthy of note is the manner in which poetry constructs either its subject or its object. The subject is Álvaro de Campos, who describes himself anaphorically as "eu, que amo a civilização moderna, eu que beijo com a alma as máquinas,/ Eu o engenheiro, eu o civilizado, eu o educado no estrangeiro" ["I, who love modern civilization, I, who kiss machines with my soul,/ I the engineer, I the civilized man, I educated abroad"]. The object, as in "Ode Triunfal", is modernity, but a modernity even more sadly aware of its history and of the fleetingness of time (Santos 2003: 185). In "Ode Marítima", as Whitman had foreseen in "Passage to India", all seas have been sailed, but the subject, alone on a deserted pier from the opening to the close of the text, finds itself aimless in sight of the violent contradictions of the present (Santos 2003: 184).

In the first section of the poem, Campos observes the entrance of a steamer in the harbour, with the bitter-sweetness that swells up in him "como uma náusea,/ Como um começar a enjoar, mas no espírito" ["as a nausea,/ As a desire to vomit, but spiritually"]. Every coming and going of ships becomes, thus, unconsciously symbolic, terribly menacing and metaphysically laden, as each and every pier is a "saudade de pedra" ["stone yearning"].

> Vem-me, não sei porquê, uma angústia recente,
> Uma névoa de sentimentos de tristeza
> Que brilha ao sol das minhas angústias relvadas
> Como a primeira janela onde a madrugada bate,
> E me envolve como uma recordação duma outra pessoa
> Que fosse misteriosamente minha.
>
> [I am hit, I don't know why, by a recent anxiety,
> A mist of sad feelings,
> Which glistens in the sun of my grassy anxieties
> Like the first window where dawn beats,
> And wraps me as if it were the memory of someone else
> Now mysteriously mine.]

When the ship sails off afar, the subject is inexplicably caught by anguish and by a mist of sadness. A sort of remembrance envelops him, belonging to someone else who is perhaps the subject itself. Then Campos sings in this manner, "o mistério de cada ida e de cada chegada,/ A dolorosa instabilidade e incompreensibilidade/ Deste impossível universo" ["the mystery of every departure and every arrival,/ the sad instability and inscrutability/ Of this impossible universe"]:

> Quando as nossas entranhas se arrepanham
> E uma vaga sensação parecida com um medo
> – O medo ancestral de se afastar e partir,
> O misterioso receio ancestral à Chegada e ao Novo –
> Encolhe-nos a pele e agonia-nos,
> E todo o nosso corpo angustiado sente,

Como se fosse a nossa alma,
Uma inexplicável vontade de poder sentir isto doutra maneira:
Uma saudade a qualquer cousa,
Uma perturbação de afeições a que vaga pátria?

[When our innards wrinkle
And a vague sensation as with a fear
– The ancestral fear of distance and of setting off,
The mysterious ancestral caution at Arrival and at the New –
Shrinks our skin and pains us,
And all our anguished body feels,
As if it were our soul,
An inexplicable wish to be able to feel this differently:
A longing for something,
Perturbed affections for some vague homeland?]

The grieving subject feels a nostalgia for something, perhaps a disquiet for a vague country, and there are moments in the Pacific Ocean when, through some suggestion learnt in school, it feels weighing on the nerves the fact that this is the vastest of oceans.

At this point, Campos makes use of terms that reveal all the contradictions of this Pessoan heteronym that we previously have called "futurable", yes, but not "futurist":

E eu, que amo a civilização moderna, eu que beijo com a alma as máquinas,
Eu o engenheiro, eu o civilizado, eu o educado no estrangeiro,
Gostaria de ter outra vez ao pé da minha vista só veleiros e barcos de
    madeira,
De não saber doutra vida marítima que a antiga vida dos mares!

[And I, who love modern civilization, I, who kiss machines with my soul,
I the engineer, I the civilized man, I educated abroad,
I would like to see once again only yachts and wooden boats,
To know of maritime life nothing but the ancient life of the seas!]

The engineer trained in Glasgow celebrates modernity, but would still love to have before his eyes sailing vessels of wood, the ancient life of the seas. According to the poet, the seas of that time were the "Distância Absoluta,/ O Puro Longe, liberto do peso do Actual" ["Absolute Distance,/ the Pure Afar, free from the pain of the Present"]. Abandoning himself in a sigh, Campos mentally retraces that "better life", those greater seas, for then one navigated more slowly and with mystery, as they were far less known.

We find the selfsame nostalgia for the past also in the very first lines of "Passage to India". Here, Whitman, singing the great successes of the present and the marvels of modernity (engineering works, railways, telegraphic cables that traverse the seas), also sang the praises of an infinitely great past:

> The Past! The Past! The Past!
> The Past – the dark unfathom'd retrospect!
> The teeming gulf – the sleepers and the shadows!
> The Past – the infinite greatness of the past!
> For what is present after all but a growth out of the past?

The present, for the Long Island poet, is like a projectile that originated in the past and that the past has made explode. It is, therefore, inconceivable that there can be an exaltation of the modern that is not, simultaneously, a eulogy of the past.

In "Ode Marítima", Campos interrupts his reflection on the "antiga vida dos mares", showing a desire that is typically *sensacionista*:

> Todos os mares, todos os estreitos, todas as baías, todos os golfos,
> Queria apertá-los ao peito, senti-los bem e morrer!

> [All seas, all straits, all bays, all gulfs,
> I would like to squeeze them to my breast, feel them and die!]

The poet not only aspires to tightening to his heart and feeling all seas, all straits and all gulfs, but also begins to feel pervaded by the "delírio das cousas marítimas" ["delirium for maritime things"]; the lapping of the water wraps up his senses; the pier and its atmosphere penetrate Campos physically and he starts to dream. Words such as "olhar" ["to look"] and "ver" ["to see"], punctuating the first part of the text, later give way to "sonhar" ["to dream"] and "sentir" ["to feel"]. This distancing from material reality was present in "Passage to India" too. In the initial sections of the Whitman poem, the experience of reality was transmitted thus:

> I see the plentiful larkspur and wild onions, the barren, colorless, sage-deserts,
> I see in glimpses afar or towering immediately above me the great mountains, I see the Wind river and the Wahsatch mountains,
> I see the Monument mountain and the Eagle's Nest
> [...]
> I see the Humboldt range, I thread the valley and cross the river,
> I see the clear waters of Lake Tahoe, I see forests of majestic pines...

Successively, Whitman begins to appeal to his soul itself, questioning it and exposing his own doubts ("Ah who shall soothe these feverish children?/ Who justify these restless explorations?/ Who speak the secret of impassive earth?). Pessoa demonstrated himself, in the many annotations written on his copy of *Leaves of Grass*, to be sensible to the Whitmanesque anaphoric use of verbs. In the poem "The Ox-Tamer", for example, Pessoa underlined all six recurrences in which the verb "to see" appeared.

In "Ode Marítima", the Pessoan heteronym evokes the figure of the English sailor Jim Barnes:

> Foste tu [...]
> Que me ensinaste esse grito antiquíssimo, inglês...
>
> [It was you [...]
> Who taught me that ancient English cry...]

Barnes's cry ("Ahó ó-ó ó-ó-ó-ó-ó -----yyyy... Schooner ahó-ó-ó ó-ó-ó-ó-ó----yyyy"), heard by Campos as in a hallucination, wakes the poet up "to something" and the tone of the ode assumes a decidedly more futuristic character. The engineer is unexpectedly moved by an unstoppable instinct to leave, to set off towards the open sea, taken by the squall:

Ah, seja como for, seja para onde for, partir!
Largar por aí fora, pelas ondas, pelo perigo, pelo mar,
Ir para Longe, ir para Fora, para a Distância Abstracta,
Indefinidamente, pelas noites misteriosas e fundas,
Levado, como a poeira, plos ventos, plos vendavais!
Ir, ir, ir, ir de vez!

[Ah, whatever happens, wherever, to depart!
To move far off, over the waves, through dangers, through the sea,
To go Far Away, Far Off, into the Abstract Distance,
Undefined, through deep and mysterious nights,
Carried, like dust, by the winds, by the storms!
To go, go, go, go at once!]

The desire to be far away, towards the Absolute Distance, had already been expressed in section IX of "Passage to India". Here, Whitman exhorted his soul to cast anchor, cut the hawsers and unfurl the sails in order to travel where no sailor had yet dared to venture:

Passage, immediate passage! the blood burns in my veins!
Away O Soul! hoist instantly the anchor!
Cut the hawsers – haul out – shake out every sail!
Have we not stood here like trees in the ground long enough?
Have we not grovel'd and dazed ourselves with books long enough?
Sail forth – steer for the deep waters only,
Reckless O Soul, exploring, I with thee, and thou with me,
For we are bound where mariner has not yet dared to go,
And we will risk the ship, ourselves and all.
O my brave soul!
O farther farther sail!

O daring joy, but safe! are they not all the seas of God?
O farther, farther, farther sail!

These lines evoke, too, another poem of Walt Whitman in the section "Children of Adam" of *Leaves of Grass*, the title of which is "One Hour to Madness and Joy":

O something unprov'd! something in a trance!
To escape utterly from others' anchors and holds!
To drive free! to love free! to dash reckless and dangerous!
To court destruction with taunts, with invitations!
To ascend, to leap to the heavens of the love indicated to me!
To rise thither with my inebriate soul!
To be lost if it must be so!
To feed the remainder of life with one hour of fullness and freedom!
With one brief hour of madness and joy.

Here, the poet celebrates the ecstasy of escaping completely from every anchor and every hold, the perdition throughout a brief hour of fullness and liberty.

Again, in "Ode Marítima", Campos, aware of the prior Whitman text, gives an unmistakably personal imprint to his own composition, singing that masochism through mechanisms already present in "Ode Triunfal". In this case, the poet seeks to be crucified, lacerated, struck, killed to the sound of the waves, in order to bring to Death a soul overflowing with Sea:

Sim, sim, sim... Crucificai-me nas navegações
E as minhas espáduas gozarão a minha cruz!
Atai-me às viagens como a postes
E a sensação dos postes entrará pela minha espinha
E eu passarei a senti-los num vasto espasmo passivo!
Fazei o que quiserdes de mim, logo que seja nos mares,
Sobre conveses, ao som de vagas,
Que me rasgueis, mateis, firais!

[Yes, yes, yes... Crucify me on navigations
And my shoulders will revel in my cross!
Tie me to voyages as if to stakes
And the sensation of the stakes will enter through my spine
And I will feel them in a vast, passive ecstasy!
Do what you will of me, as long as it's at sea,
On ship decks, to the sound of waves,
Wound me, kill me, rip me open!]

He hopes, further, that they tear off his skin and nail it down on the keels, so that he can "sentir a dor dos pregos e nunca deixar de sentir" ["feel the pain of the nails and never stop feeling it"]; that they yank out his eyes and grind them into the deck with their feet; that they break his bones against the walls.

Fustiguem-me atado aos mastros, fustiguem-me!
A todos os ventos de todas as latitudes e longitudes
Derramem meu sangue sobre as águas arremessadas
Que atravessam o navio, o tombadilho, de lado a lado,
Nas vascas bravas das tormentas!

[Tie me to the masts and trash me, trash me!
To all the winds of all latitudes and longitudes
Spill my blood over the raging waters
Crossing the deck, the poop deck, from side to side,
In the wild convulsions of the storms!]

The poet proceeds, thus, enumerating a series of rough images typical of that "word binge", of that intoxication of language, at which Brown hinted: sunken ships, blood on the seas, decks full of blood, fragments of corpses, cut off fingers, heads of children here and there. Campos comes, then, to exclaim:

Fogo, fogo, fogo, dentro de mim!
Sangue! sangue! sangue! sangue!
Explode todo o meu cérebro!

Parte-se-me o mundo em vermelho!
Estoiram-me com o som de amarras as veias!

[Fire, fire, fire, inside me!
Blood! Blood! Blood! Blood!
My whole brain explodes!
The world splits into red!
My veins snap with the sound of cables!]

Whilst the world of Campos fragments into redness, the poet introduces the theme of piracy. The *sensacionista* heteronym appeals to the pirates to love him, hate him and take him with them. Giving voice to the tendency that we have already defined as intersexual, the poet turns thus to the pirates:

Vossa fúria, vossa crueldade como falam ao sangue
Dum corpo de mulher que foi meu outrora e cujo cio sobrevive!

[Your fury, your cruelty, how they speak to the blood
Of a woman's body that once was mine and whose lust has survived!]

The ferocity of those men speaks to the blood of a woman's body that Campos claims once to have been his and of whom still today survives the rut, the aforementioned "cio". Whitman, in the poem "Whoever You are, Holding Me now in Hand", affirmed: "[For] I am the new husband, and I am the comrade". The Pessoan heteronym continues, instead, to proclaim repeatedly his own passivity:

Ser o meu corpo passivo a mulher-todas-as-mulheres
Que foram violadas, mortas, feridas, rasgadas pelos piratas!
Ser no meu ser subjugado a fêmea que tem de ser deles
E sentir tudo isso – todas estas coisas duma só vez – pela espinha!

[Let my passive body be the woman-all-women
That were violated, killed, wounded, torn apart by pirates!

Let into my subjugated being the female who is to be theirs
And let me feel all this – all these things at once – down my spine!]

Moved by what Pessoa termed the *mal de Whitman*, Campos expresses a longing to be the woman-all-women. Torture becomes, for the engineer, a cure ("Ah, torturai-me para me curardes!" ["Ah, torture me to cure me!"]). For this reason, he asks to be knelt down and humiliated, be rendered a slave and a "thing" in the hands of his lords and masters.

Successively, we bump into what we have already seen in "Saudação a Walt Whitman", Campos's identification in and with the other. In "Saudação", we read, "Eu, Álvaro de Campos, [...]/ Eu sou Tu". In the case of "Ode Marítima", we find:

Agora, no auge conciso de sonhar o que vós fazíeis,
Perco-me todo de mim, já não vos pertenço, sou vós,
A minha feminilidade que vos acompanha é ser as vossas almas!

[Now, in the concise climax of dreaming what you were doing,
I lose myself completely, I don't belong to you anymore, I am you,
My femininity, that accompanies you, is being your very souls!]

At the culmination of dreaming the prowess of the pirates, Campos declares that he no longer belongs to those seamen, rather he *is* those men. Here is a classic example of the Pessoan "outrar-se" – a phenomenon that is present, to a lesser degree, also in Whitman, whose following lines Pessoa has singled out:

> Agonies are one of my changes of garments,
> I do not ask the wounded person how he feels, I myself become the wounded person,
> My hurts turn livid upon me as I lean on a cane and observe.

"Song of Myself", in *Leaves of Grass*, p. 75.

Turning to "Ode Marítima", suddenly, as if waking up from sleep, the naval engineer is invaded by an "inexplicável ternura" ["inexplicable tenderness"] and by the regret for having dreamed about being a buccaneer. He repents of having raped so many victims and takes his distance from what he was until just a moment before:

Ah, como pude eu pensar, sonhar aquelas cousas?
Que longe estou do que fui há uns momentos!

[Ah, how could I have thought, dreamt those things?
How far I am from what I was just moments ago!]

We know that Campos is hardly new to this kind of interruption. One can spot the presence of such a suspension of discourse also in an undated text, the first lines of which are:

Gostava de gostar de gostar.
Um momento... Dá-me de ali um cigarro,
Do maço em cima da mesa de cabeceira.
Continua...

[I would like to like to like.
One moment... Give me a cigarette from there,
From the pack on the bedside table.
Go on...]

In "Insónia" (1929), the poet, lying on the bed, has the strength to do nothing other than write lines "escritos no dia seguinte":

Sim, escritos no dia seguinte.
Todos os versos são sempre escritos no dia seguinte.

[Yes, written the following day.
All the verses are always written the following day.]

For Pessoa, interruption constitutes the base of poetry. In the essay "O Homem de Porlock", published in the journal *Fradique* in 1934,[12] the poet reconstructed the history of the poem "Kubla Khan" by Coleridge – a work that, though fragmentary, was considered by Pessoa as one of the most extraordinary poems of English literature. Coleridge had staged what, on a lesser scale, was common to all poets: indeed, all, even if awake when they compose verses, compose in a dream, and all, even if they do not receive any visits, are visited from the inside by the man from Porlock, "the interrupter". The essence of the writer, in the moment in which he tries to express it, suffers from the interruption of that visitor who is the author himself, the external individual that every writer carries inside the self. Between the beginning and the end of the text, every poet has to welcome this visitor, who will impede him from writing down his verses. The consequence is that from artists there only survives something which is not well defined, that would have been the expression of a soul, if only it had been realized. As a result of this reflection, Pessoa claimed that there remains only the opening and the closure of something lost – the *disjecta membra* of every poet and every man.

The poetics of interruption, intended as a paradoxical manifestation of the human desire for impossible totality and beauty, link Pessoa to the author of *Leaves of Grass* who, in section XXXVIII of "Song of Myself", made a clean break, exclaiming:

Enough! enough! enough!
Somehow I have been stunn'd. Stand back!

The selfsame behaviour is to be found again in "Out of the Cradle Endlessly Rocking", in which the poet interrupts a comforting sea shanty, and in "As I Ebb'd with the Ocean of Life", where Whitman lets his "real Me" break through to denounce the arrogance of the "barbaric yawp" of the writer himself.

In "Ode Marítima", Campos suddenly perceives that his dreams are vanishing and that some dew is beading his excitement ("O frescor nocturno no meu oceano interior!" ["The nocturnal freshness in my inner ocean!"]). It is

---

[12] Fernando Pessoa, "O Homem de Porlock", in *Fradique 1*(Feb. 15, 1934), p. 8.

thus possible to affirm that for every poetic dream, as for the erotic dream, a man of Porlock will knock at the door of the imagination of the subject.

Once again in the present, Campos is caressed by reminiscences of a distant childhood and becomes aware of the fact that nothing will give him back his past. When he tries to re-evoke the violence of the pirates and the bloodshed, he is no longer able, imagination refuses to accompany him. The cry of the mariner Jim Barnes is mixed and overcome by the echo of the lullabies that his aunt had sung to him when he was little. This is how Campos returns to the reality of the pier: "Eis outra vez o mundo real, tão bondoso para os nervos!" ["Here once more the real world, so bounteous for the nerves!"].

The poet's inner fly-wheel slows and the heteronym can focus once again on the ships that come and go from the harbour, feeling natural and discreet gentlemanly sentiments, unrelated to delirium. And while the last steamer moves off, Campos observes its passage with a curious and grateful affection and feels restored to life.

Also in "Ode Marítima", we witness the re-entry into the ranks of an Álvaro de Campos incapable of assuming revolutionary positions for any longer than that hour of madness and joy of which Whitman spoke ("One Hour to Madness and Joy"). It is Edwin Honig's opinion, one with which we agree, that in the poem Whitman's presence emerges everywhere. Among the phantoms that hide in the mist and in the breeze of "Ode Marítima", there would not only be Jim Barnes crying out his sea shanty on the pirates on the chest of the dead man – "Yo-ho-ho and a bottle of rum" – but also the spiritual guide of Walt, tuned an octave or two higher (Honig 1988: 392). It is legitimate to ask if that "grito antiquíssimo inglês" ["most ancient English yell"] that Campos has learned from Barnes was not the very "barbaric yawp" of Walt Whitman.

"Ode Marítima" is, we suggest, amongst the works that we have looked at, the one in which the defeat of the poet is most evident. Indeed, far from being a futurist poem, "Ode Marítima" would be neither sad nor monotonous: according to Eduardo Lourenço, it would be Sadness itself (Lourenço 1973: 130). To be the singer of progress and modernity, Campos exalts the voyaging imagination in a precarious and fictitious way. The rapid coming back to reality and to its anxieties brings confirmation to the poet of the uselessness of every departure. Yet, the young Campos had already come to this conclusion some time before, when, crossing the Suez Canal, he wrote "Opiário" ["Opiary"]. In this poem, later published in *Orpheu*, we read that, according to the poet, it is not worth the effort of being in the Orient, in India, or in China:

> Eu acho que não vale a pena ter
> Ido ao Oriente e visto a Índia e a China.
> A terra é semelhante e pequenina
> E há só uma maneira de viver.
>
> [I find that it is not worth having gone
> To the Orient and seen India and China.
> The earth is similar and small
> And there is only one way to live.]

Paradoxically, Álvaro de Campos, the Pessoan heteronym who has travelled the most, finds that but one journey is truly stimulating: the last one, the definitive departure. Among the unpublished texts of Campos discovered since 1990, a poem was discovered, entitled "A partida" ["The departure"] (Perrone-Moisés 2014: 174), in which the poet prepares himself to sail towards Death without expectations, but ready to witness whatever prodigy is to be found on the other side of the world:

> Partirei para aquele teu aspecto que a Morte deve revelar-me
> Com o coração confrangido, a alma ansiosa, o olhar vago,
> E toda a consciência da aventura pondo-me ondas no sangue...
> Eu partirei para a Morte nada esperando encontrar
> Mas disposto a ver coisas prodigiosas do outro lado do Mundo.
>
> [I shall leave for that aspect of yours that Death must reveal to me
> With my anguished heart, my anxious soul, my vague gaze,
> And the whole consciousness of adventure sending waves into my blood...
> I shall depart for Death hoping to encounter nothing
> But disposed to see prodigious things from the other side of the World.]

Wearing futurist clothes, the dying Campos will make this definitive journey in a divine car, in a bed turned into Montgolfier or in a train wagon.

We have seen how the proper comprehension of the creative reception of Whitman on the part of Pessoa-Campos requires a reading of "Saudação a Walt Whitman" conjointly with the two odes "Triunfal" and "Marítima". We shall now go on to consider how Pessoa responded to Whitman's appeal contained in "Poets to Come" through the heteronym Alberto Caeiro.

Of Caeiro, we shall say only that he was born in 1889 (one year before Campos and one year after Pessoa) and died of tuberculosis in 1915. We limit ourselves to this scant information in order to support the heteronymic game of Pessoa, who attributed to Caeiro the following lines, contained in one of his *Poemas Inconjuntos* [*Uncollected Poems*]: "Se, depois de eu morrer, quiserem escrever a minha biografia,/ Não há nada mais simples./ Tem só duas datas – a da minha nascença e a da minha morte./ Entre uma e outra coisa todos os dias são meus" ["If, after I die, someone wants to write my biography,/ There is nothing simpler./ It has just two dates – the day I was born and the day I died./ Between the two, all the days are mine"] (Pessoa 1999: 222). For the rest, not much is known of this solitary and contemplative heteronym, who led an existence distant from all clamour and free from attachments of the heart: he led his brief life in a village in Ribatejo, where he had retired because of his delicate health. It was exactly in the hinterland that, during a walk, Caeiro had met Álvaro de Campos. That accidental encounter so deeply marked Campos that he became at once a devoted disciple. *Mestre* [*Master*] Caeiro also brought together, amongst his followers, Fernando Pessoa (in whom he appeared on 8 March 1914) and Ricardo Reis (the Pessoan heteronym more imbued with Classicism and Hellenism).

Of the Master, there remain the short poems of the *Guardador de Rebanhos*, the six poems of *O Pastor Amoroso* [*The Shepherd in Love*] and the compositions of *Poemas Inconjuntos*. The poetry of Caeiro is a prime example of what many critics would call "objective" lyrical poetry, or also "pure" poetry, that is, a poetry unchained from history (space and time) and free from the burden of morals, compassion and finalized engagement. The art of Caeiro, which coincides with an innocent visual transparency, presents itself as a kind of "superior" imagination that Ramalho describes in these terms: "deconceptualized, intellectually detached, radically independent, and endowed with the capacity to look and see without thinking" (Santos 2003: 215).

In an extended reflection jotted down by Pessoa around 1917, we read that Caeiro was "strange and terribly, appallingly new" – he was perhaps "too new" – and astonished the reader with his genial and innovative contribution. The Master felt no tenderness for the things that surrounded him and hardly any affection for his own feelings: "Here we touch his great originality, his almost inconceivable objectiveness (objectivity). He sees things with the eyes only, not with the mind. He does not let any thoughts arise when he looks at a flower" (Pessoa 1996: 335).

Very far from seeing sermons in stones, Caeiro would not even have conceived that a stone was the beginning of a lesson. The only lesson that a stone could give is that it exists. This way of looking at rocks and flowers may be considered completely unpoetic. The astounding characteristic linked to Caeiro is that, from these sensations, or rather from this absence of sensations, he made poetry.

> Put it to yourselves: what do you think of a stone when you look at it without thinking about it? This comes to this: what do you think of a stone when you don't think about it at all? The question is quite absurd, of course. The strange point about it is that all Caeiro's poetry is based upon that sentiment that you find it impossible to represent to yourself as able to exist. (Pessoa 1996: 335)

We know that Álvaro de Campos labelled the Master as *sensacionista* and that this did not please Caeiro. Yet, according to Pessoa, no other definition better captures Caeiro's attitude: his poetry would be absolutely sensationist, because in it "Sensation is all [...] and thought is a disease". By "sensation", however, Caeiro intended the feeling of things as they are, without the supplement of introspective elements, conventions or sentiments. The disciple Campos was a *sensacionista* too, but he conceived sensations in a subjective way. For him, feeling was all and the best thing was "sentir tudo de todas as maneiras" ["feeling everything in every way"]. Campos was the "undisciplined child of sensation". Yet, Caeiro had a discipline:

> Caeiro has no ethics except simplicity. [...] Álvaro de Campos has no shadow of an ethics; he is non-moral, if not positively immoral, for, of course, according to his theory it is natural that he should love the stronger better than the weak sensations, and the strong sensations are at least all selfish and occasionally the sensations of cruelty and lust. (Pessoa 1996: 335)

Pessoa concluded his reflection by explaining that a pure sensationist like Caeiro obviously could not follow any religion, as religion has nothing to do with the immediacy of sensation.

In the same text, we read that, despite his incomparable innovations, Caeiro could be placed near some – few – poets, but that Walt Whitman was certainly the one he was most like:

> The very few poets to whom Caeiro may be compared, either because he merely reminds, or might remind, us of them, or because he may be conceived of as having been influenced by them, whether we think it seriously or not, are Whitman, Francis Jammes and Teixeira de Pascoaes. He resembles Whitman most. (Pessoa 1996: 335)

In fact, the impact of Whitman's poetry on Caeiro seems strong: both poets aspired to find their own individuality. Caeiro, as poet of true sensations, owes to Whitman the tendency to observe nature through an apparently innocent gaze and to accept reality in its plurality.

In one of the *Poemas Inconjuntos* (which begins with "Dizes-me: tu és mais alguma coisa" ["You say: you are something more"]), the Master asks himself whether he is "more" than a stone or a plant. The answer is that he is "different", because he does not know what is "more" or "less".

> Sei que a pedra é real, e que a planta existe.
> Sei isto porque elas existem.
> Sei isto porque os meus sentidos mo mostram.

Sei que sou real também.
Sei isto porque os meus sentidos mo mostram,
Embora com menos clareza que me mostram a pedra e a planta.

[I know the stone is real and the plant exists.
I know it because they exist.
I know it because my senses show it to me.
I know I am real too.
I know it because my senses show it to me,
Though less clearly than they show me the stone and the plant.]

The poet knows that the stone and the plant are real just because, in fact, they exist and his senses have shown that to him. For the very same reason, the poet too knows himself to be real. It is the same attitude of placid acceptance that we find in the short poems of the *Guardador de Rebanhos*. Here, from text XXI, we learn that what is necessary is to be natural and calm, to feel as one who looks and to think as one who is walking:

O que é preciso é ser-se natural e calmo
Na felicidade ou na infelicidade,
Sentir como quem olha,
Pensar como quem anda,
E quando se vai morrer, lembrar-se de que o dia morre,
E que o poente é belo e é bela a noite que fica...
Assim é e assim seja...

[What matters is to be natural and calm,
In happiness and in unhappiness,
To feel as one looking,
To think as one walking,
And when we are about to die, remember that each day dies,
And that sunset is beautiful and beautiful is the night that remains...
Thus it is and thus let it be...]

The sight of something is sufficient proof of its existence. Insisting on going beyond is to have pain in the eyes, as Caeiro maintains in poem II of the *Guardador de Rebanhos*:

Pensar é não compreender...
O Mundo não se fez para pensarmos nele
(Pensar é estar doente dos olhos)

[To think is not to understand...
The World was not made for us to think about it
(To think is to be ill in the eyes)]

As the world was not made for us to think about it, to think is not to comprehend. Saint-Exupéry will say that, "L'essentiel est invisible pour les yeux" ["What is essential is invisible to the eye"]. Caeiro affirms that "O essencial é saber ver,/ Saber ver sem estar a pensar" ["What is essential is to know how to see,/ To see without thinking"], but this demands a deep study, an authentic apprenticeship to unlearn.[13] Talking about the soul of stones, flowers and rivers is to attribute to natural elements ideas that actually they can not possess. Nature is free from interiority, otherwise it would not be Nature:

Falar da alma das pedras, das flores, dos rios,
É falar de si próprio e dos seus falsos pensamentos.
[...]
Por mim, escrevo a prosa dos meus versos
E fico contente,
Porque sei que compreendo a Natureza por fora;
E não a compreendo por dentro
Porque a Natureza não tem dentro;
Senão não era a Natureza.

---

[13] *O Guardador de Rebanhos*, poem XXIV.

[Talking about the soul of stones, flowers, rivers
Is talking about oneself and one's false thoughts.
[...]
As for me, I write the prose of my verses
And I am content,
Because I know I understand Nature on the outside;
And I do not understand it within
Because Nature has no within;
Otherwise it would not be Nature.] [14]

In section VI of "Song of Myself", we read that a child turns to Whitman, asking him what was grass. The poet, however, does not know how to respond, because he knows no more that his questioner:

A child said What is the grass? fetching it to me with full hands;
How could I answer the child? I do not know what it is any more than he.

In the same text, section XIII, we come across lines that sound somewhat familiar to us:

And do not call the tortoise unworthy because she is not something else,
And the jay in the woods never studied the gamut, yet trills pretty well to me,
And the look of the bay mare shames silliness out of me.

Just as Caeiro cannot judge whether a flower is "more" than a man, in the same manner Whitman does not consider living beings more or less "worthy", just different. Further on, in section XXXI of "Song of Myself", it becomes obvious how greatly Whitman's verse impinges on that of Caeiro:

I believe a leaf of grass is no less than the journey-work of the stars,
And the pismire is equally perfect, and a grain of sand, and the egg of the wren,

---

[14] *O Guardador de Rebanhos*, poem XXVIII.

And the tree-toad is a chef-d'oeuvre for the highest,
And the running blackberry would adorn the parlors of heaven,
And the narrowest hinge in my hand puts to scorn all machinery,
And the cow crunching with depress'd head surpasses any statue,
And a mouse is miracle enough to stagger sextillions of infidels.

These are lines that precede those of section XLIV which Pessoa underlined:

> I do not call one greater and one smaller,
> That which fills its period and place is equal to any.

"Song of Myself", in *Leaves of Grass*, p. 88.

"Tudo é como é e assim é que é" ["Everything is as it is and so it is that is"] maintains Caeiro in poem XXIII of the *Guardador de Rebanhos*:

Porque tudo é como é e assim é que é,
e eu aceito, e nem agradeço,
para não parecer que penso nisso...

[Because everything is as it is and so it is that is,
And I accept it, and do not give thanks,
For not appearing to be thinking of this...]

Everything is found in its right place, therefore. It is that superior calm that emerges in the parentheses of "Song of Myself":

(The moth and the fish-eggs are in their place,
The bright suns I see and the dark suns I cannot see are in their place,
The palpable is in its place and the impalpable is in its place.)

For a long time the planet has been rolling, the rain has been falling and the grass has been growing – writes the author of *Leaves of Grass* in "Song of

Exposition" – and there is no reason why this should change:

> Long and long has the grass been growing,
> Long and long has the rain been falling,
> Long has the globe been rolling around.

In Whitman, body and soul, material and spiritual, melt together without one element prevailing over the other. In section VI of "Starting from Paumanok", we read:

> I will make the poems of materials, for I think they are to be the most spiritual poems,
> And I will make the poems of my body and of mortality,
> For I think I shall then supply myself with the poems of my soul and of immortality.

It is a disposition similar to one we find in "Song of Myself". Denied here is the supremacy of the soul over the body, or that of the body over the soul:

> I have said that the soul is not more than the body,
> and I have said that the body is not more than the soul,
> and nothing, not god, is greater to one than one's self is.

Therefore, the subject can laze and put itself at ease, contemplating the spiny summer grass in perfect communion with his soul. The grass is as welcome, for the North American writer, as a maternal lap, like the colourless beard of ancients, and the fields are for Whitman like a handkerchief that the Lord let fall on purpose, which perhaps has the name of its owner in a corner:

> I loaf and invite my soul,
> I lean and loaf at my ease observing a spear of summer grass.

There are no verses that can sufficiently express the joy of lying on the lawn. Álvaro de Campos is also aware of that and, in "A Passagem das Horas", affirms that there are no gestures of pleasure as worthy as that of rolling about among daisies and grass. Only by biting a tuft of grass may one understand what verses cannot express:

> Não há gestos de prazer pelo mundo que valham
> A alegria estupenda de quem não tem outro modo de a exprimir
> Que rolar-se pelo chão entre ervas e malmequeres
> E misturar-se com terra até sujar o fato e o cabelo...
> Não há versos que possam dar isto...
> Arranquem um (...) de erva, trinquem-na e perceber-me-ão,
> Perceberão completamente o que eu incompletamente exprimo.

> [There are no gestures of pleasure across the world that are worth
> The stupendous joy of whomsoever has no other way to express it
> Except rolling around on the ground amongst grasses and daisies
> And mingling with earth until soiling his suit and his hair...
> There are no verses that can transmit this...
> Pull up a (...) of grass, bite it and you will understand me,
> You will understand completely what I incompletely express.]

In comparable manner, Alberto Caeiro concludes poem IX of the *Guardador de Rebanhos* by describing the happiness resulting from stretching out on the fields with eyes closed:

> Por isso quando num dia de calor
> Me sinto triste de gozá-lo tanto,
> E me deito ao comprido na erva,
> E fecho os olhos quentes,
> Sinto todo o meu corpo deitado na realidade,
> Sei a verdade e sou feliz.

> [That is why on a hot day
> I feel sad from enjoying it so much,
> And I lie in the long grass,
> And I close my warm eyes,

I feel my whole body laid upon reality,
I know the truth and am happy.]

Whilst the subject rests on grass, he is permeable to every revelation. Thus, in section V of "Song of Myself", Whitman evokes the peace and transcendental knowledge that suddenly form around the self, rendering it conscious of brotherhood with entire creation:

> Swiftly arose and spread around me the peace and knowledge that pass all the argument of the earth,
> And I know that the hand of God is the promise of my own,
> And I know that the spirit of God is the brother of my own,
> And that all the men ever born are also my brothers, and the women my sisters and lovers,
> And that a keelson of the creation is love,
> And limitless are leaves stiff or dropping in the fields,
> And brown ants in the little wells beneath them,
> And mossy scabs of the worm fence, heap'd stones, elder, mullein and poke-weed.

A similar epiphany is lived by Alberto Caeiro's persona in poem XXXVIII of the *Guardador de Rebanhos*. Here, the *Mestre*'s projection, observing the sun, feels a sense of fraternity towards all men, because everyone, even if distant, at least once a day looks at the sun. A strong link is thus forged, too, with primitive man who, even before adoring God and morality, saw the sun rise and set:

> Bendito seja o mesmo sol de outras terras
> Que faz meus irmãos todos os homens
> Porque todos os homens, um momento no dia, o olham como eu,
> E nesse puro momento
> Todo limpo e sensível
> Regressam lacrimosamente
> E com um suspiro que mal sentem

Ao Homem verdadeiro e primitivo
Que via o Sol nascer e ainda o não adorava.
Porque isso é natural – mais natural
Que adorar o ouro e Deus
E a arte e a moral...

[Blessed be the same sun of other lands
Which turns into my brothers all men
Because all men, once a day, look at it as I do,
And in that pure moment
All clear and sensitive
Go back tearfully
And with a sigh hardly felt
To the true primitive Man
Who saw the Sun rise up and did not yet adore it.
Because that is natural – more natural
Than worshipping gold and God
And art and morals...]

Although in Caeiro the Whitman legacy is obvious (that impression of absolute communion between man and nature, that respect for sensations), we also find that the *sensacionismo* of the Pessoan heteronym moves a little away from that of the author of *Leaves of Grass*. Indeed, whilst Whitman constantly sought to establish connections between the observed object and all the others (soul, Universe, God), the *Mestre* attempted to isolate the object from all the rest and from all the sensations that were not part of it. The Long Island poet wrote, in the poem "On the beach at night alone": "A vast similitude interlocks all,/ All spheres, grown, ungrown, small, large, suns moons, planets".

Crucially, Caeiro rarely refers to God:

Só a Natureza é divina e ela não é divina...

[Only Nature is divine and it is not divine…][15]

Whitman, on the contrary, felt, inseparably, an inner and outer divinity:

> Divine am I inside and out, and I make holy whatever I touch or am touch'd from…[16]

Of Caeiro, in "Notas Para a Recordação do Meu Mestre Caeiro", Álvaro de Campos said, "O meu mestre Caeiro não era um pagão: era o paganismo" ["My master Caeiro was not a pagan: he was paganism"]. In fact, in the Master's poetry, what is totally absent is any meditation on the mystery of things. For Caeiro, the only mystery was that there was anyone who thought of mystery, and the only inner meaning of things was that there was no inner meaning at all.[17] The heteronym could not believe in God because he had never seen him. "Se ele quisesse que eu acreditasse nele" – wrote Caeiro – "sem dúvida que viria falar comigo" ["If he wanted me to believe in him, he would undoubtedly come to speak with me"].

Famously, poem V of the *Guardador de Rebanhos* opens thus:

> Há metafísica bastante em não pensar em nada.

> [There is metaphysics enough in not thinking about anything.]

This line probably harks back to "Song of Myself", in which Whitman confessed:

> A morning-glory at my windows satisfies me more than the metaphysics of books.

In this respect, it is worth reading too a text from the "Calamus" section entitled "The Base of all Metaphysics". Here, at the end of a class, an old

---

[15] *O Guardador de Rebanhos*, poem XXVII.
[16] "Song of Myself".
[17] *O Guardador de Rebanhos*, poem V.

professor, after having taught Kant, Fichte, Schelling, Hegel, Plato and Socrates, wants to reveal to his students the foundation and also the end of all metaphysics:

> I see reminiscent to-day those Greek and Germanic systems,
> See the philosophies all – Christian churches and tenets see,
> Yet underneath Socrates clearly see – and underneath Christ the divine I see,
> The dear love of man for his comrade – the attraction of friend to friend,
> Of the well-married husband and wife – of children and parents,
> Of city for city, and land for land.

Further, it is instructive to look at a poem, "I Sit and Look Out", from the "By the Roadside" section of *Leaves of Grass*. The text opens thus: "I sit and look out upon all the sorrows of the world, and upon all oppression and shame". Successively, there is an enumeration of abuses of power to which the subject was a witness: women who have been ill treated by their husbands, the strain caused by battles, by plagues and by tyranny, the offences and the humiliations suffered by labourers, by the poor and by African Americans. Whitman closes the text with the admission:

> All these – all the meanness and agony without end I sitting look out upon,
> See, hear, and I'm silent.

In these lines, it is possible to glimpse and to recognize immediately a foreshadowing of Alberto Caeiro, the great spectator of what surrounds him, who, from the opening of poem I of the *Guardador de Rebanhos*, appears simply seated contemplating nature without wanting to interpret it:

> Toda a paz da Natureza sem gente
> Vem sentar-se a meu lado.
>
> [All the peace of Nature without people
> Comes to sit by my side.]

In the same poem, we read: "Quando me sento a escrever versos/ [...] Escrevo versos num papel que está no meu pensamento..." ["When I sit down to write verse/ [...] I write verse on a paper that is in my thought..."]. Further on, Caeiro turns to all his future readers, wishing them "sol/ E chuva, quando a chuva é precisa,/ E que as suas casas tenham/ Ao pé duma janela aberta/ Uma cadeira predilecta/ Onde se sentem, lendo os meus versos" ["sun/ And rain, when rain is needed,/ And may their houses have/ Next to an open window/ A favourite chair/ To sit in, reading my verse"]. The image of the sitting poet reappears in one of the *Poemas Inconjuntos*, whose first line is "Verdade, mentira, certeza, incerteza..." ["Truth, lies, certainty, uncertainty..."]. Here, the Master affirms "Estou sentado num degrau alto e tenho as mãos apertadas/ Sobre o mais alto dos joelhos cruzados" ["I am sitting on a high step with my hands clasped/ on the higher of my crossed knees"]. These lines reveal much about the attitude of the heteronym, a tendency of always being a witness and rarely a participant in what happens around him. It is not accidentally that Caeiro is often put in a detached position, from which he can observe nature in a privileged way without allowing himself to be involved in it (very often, the *Mestre* looks on reality through a window or, as in the case of the poetry of the *Poemas Inconjuntos*, cited above, being seated on a high step).

It may be asked how the innocent shepherd poet had learned all he knew and who was the master who had revealed to him the science of perception. According to Brown, it is possible to find an answer to these questions only once the underlying presence of Whitman between the lines of the *Guardador de Rebanhos* is acknowledged (Brown 1991: 9). Recognizing the presence-absence of the North American writer in the texts of the keeper of flocks would be the key to solving the mystery of Caeiro. In this sense, poem VIII merits special attention. It refers to the dream-vision Caeiro had of Jesus Christ: it is told that the baby Jesus fell from Paradise, descended to earth thanks to a sunbeam and appeared to the shepherd as "o deus que faltava" ["the missing god"]. Jesus (also called "Eterna Criança" ["Eternal Child"] and "Criança Nova" ["New Child"]) was tired of having to be serious and of having to appear on the cross and die continually with a crown of thorns on his head. He was fed up with not being able to have a father and a mother like all the other babies. So, he escaped and took refuge in Caeiro's village. Only here was he allowed to run and roll in the grass, splash in pools of water, throw stones at asses, pick flowers and throw them away. Far from the Kingdom of Heaven, the Eternal Child could chase girls, who passed carrying jugs on their heads, and lift their skirts. The encounter with the New Child was of indispensable importance for Caeiro, who learned everything from Jesus:

> A mim ensinou-me tudo.
> Ensinou-me a olhar para as coisas.
> Aponta-me todas as coisas que há nas flores.
> Mostra-me como as pedras são engraçadas
> Quando a gente as tem na mão
> E olha devagar para elas.
>
> [He taught me everything.
> He taught me to look at things.
> He points out all the things that are in flowers.
> He shows me how stones are amusing
> When people have them in their hands
> And look slowly at them.]

We discover soon in poem VIII that it was precisely the constant presence of the baby Jesus that turned Caeiro into a poet, permitting every little glimpse to fill him with sensation:

> E a criança tão humana que é divina
> É esta minha quotidiana vida de poeta,
> E é porque ele anda sempre comigo que eu sou poeta sempre
> E que o meu mínimo olhar
> Me enche de sensação,
> E o mais pequeno som, seja o que for,
> Parece falar comigo.
>
> [And the child who is so human that he is divine
> Is my daily life as a poet,

And it is because he always goes with me that I am always a poet
And that my briefest glance
Fills me with sensation,
And the slightest sound, whatever it is,
Seems to be speaking with me.]

What resulted from the encounter between Caeiro and Jesus can be better understood if seen in light of the awakening of Whitman in section V of "Song of Myself". Susan Margaret Brown, and we agree with her, interprets the relationship between the Master and "the missing God" as being like the link between "Self" and "Myself" in "Song of Myself". The episode of the *Guardador de Rebanhos* would be, thus, the re-elaboration of the scene of the communion of the Bard with his own soul. The twenty lines of Whitman – which begin with "I believe in you my soul, the other I am must not abase itself to you" – could be set alongside poem VIII like a model alongside a copy.

In "Song of Myself", the poet turns to his soul, reminding her how once they laid down on grass together. At the time, the soul of the poet unbuttoned his shirt on his chest, plunged its tongue into his bared heart and laid on the man until covering his feet too. It was in that moment that peace and superior knowledge were revealed to Whitman. In poem VIII of the *Guardador de Rebanhos*, we read that Caeiro bears Jesus home in his arms and puts him to bed, undressing him slowly until he is naked. The Child sleeps in the soul of his Master, who warns him: "Quando eu morrer [...],/ Pega-me tu ao colo/ E leva-me para dentro da tua casa./ Despe o meu ser cansado e humano/ E deita-me na tua cama" ["When I'll die [...],/ Hold me tight/ And take me into your house./ Undress my tired and human self/ And lay me in your bed."]

According to what we read in "The Whitman-Pessoa Connection", in the figure of the new God of the *Guardador de Rebanhos* we find the reincarnation of Whitman. It would be Whitman, disguised as the Eternal Child, who facilitates the union of Caeiro with his soul, who inspires the song of the keeper of flocks and who enlightens its meaning. Before, we asked ourselves who the Master's master was. Now, we have reasons to believe that it is Whitman's lesson that moulded the verse of the shepherd poet. It is the long narration of poem VIII that generates the entire collection of the

Guardador de Rebanhos. Because Caeiro learns how to be a poet only thanks to the presence of the baby Jesus, without this contact (in a dream? in a vision?) there would not be the basis for the rest.

The essence of Whitman's message is about the nature of poetic identity. Let us analyze the first line of "There Was a Child Went Forth", a poem in the "Autumn Rivulets" section of *Leaves of Grass*:

> # THERE WAS A CHILD WENT FORTH
>
> THERE was a child went forth every day,
> And the first object he look'd upon, that object he became,
> And that object became part of him for the day or a certain part of the day,
> Or for many years or stretching cycles of years.

"There Was a Child Went Forth", in *Leaves of Grass*, p. 341.

Here was a verse Pessoa knew well – he had underlined it in his copy of *Leaves of Grass* – and which calls to mind the attitude of the innocent keeper of flocks. Like Whitman's child, Caeiro thus searched for his true self, his poetic "I", plunging intensely in the immediate sensation of an object.

Unleashing an interminable process according to which the continuous contact with external reality produced a constant metamorphosis of the self, Caeiro became, as Whitman before him, the object of his immediate perceptions. This tendency emerges also from the poems of orthonymic Pessoa. In "Ó praia de pescadores" (1913) we read, indeed:

E de tanto olhar o céu
Sinto-me ele – o sol me doura.

[And from looking so much at the sky
I am it – the sun gilds me.]

In "Não sei quantas almas" (1930), the Portuguese poet will declare once and for all:

Quem vê é só o que vê.

[Who sees is only what he sees.]

We may now consider a further cause for reflection by Susan Margaret Brown, itself borrowed from Roy Harvey Pearce, according to whom Caeiro represents, just like Whitman, the Adamic man, able to name the world itself and, thus, create it. In "Whitman Fermentation and the 1914 Vintage Season", we read:

> Pessoa initiates a new way of talking about selfhood; he begins to write, for the first time, in what Roy Harvey Pearce calls the "Adamic mode", a mode in which man defines the world in terms of himself. In this way, Pessoa "updated" Whitman in one of the most ingenious transformational strokes that literary history has known (Brown 1985: 108).

Apropos of the Adamic song, some pertinent reflections have been elaborated by Miguel de Unamuno in *El Espejo de la Muerte* (1930). For the Bilbao poet and philosopher, to name something means, to some degree, to possess it spiritually (Allen and Folsom 1995: 113). That is why the *incipit* of every love dialogue is "I love you, I love you so much, I love you with all my soul", but the conclusion contains only two words, albeit twice uttered: "Romeo!", "Juliet!", "Romeo!", "Juliet!". According to Unamuno, there is no greater proof of love than the repetition of the name of the beloved, savoured like honey in the mouth.

In *El Espejo de la Muerte*, the author recounts a scene which he will not forget for the rest of his life. One day, he saw three children who were holding hands. They were next to a horse and were exclaiming, very thrilled: "A horse! A horse! A horse!" (Allen and Folsom 1995: 113). They were creating that word while repeating it. For the Rector of the University of Salamanca, a similar thing had happened in the Book of Genesis (2:19-20):

> And out of the ground the LORD God formed every beast of the field,

and every fowl of the air; and brought them unto Adam to see what he would call them: and whatsoever Adam called every living creature, that was the name thereof.

And Adam gave names to all cattle, and to the fowl of the air, and to every beast of the field; but for Adam there was not found an help meet for him.

This was perhaps the first song, the song that attributed a name to the animals. At the dawn of humanity, Adam was ecstatic before the spectacle of Nature. Whitman entitled an entire section of *Leaves of Grass* "Children of Adam", proclaiming himself "chanter of Adamic songs".[18] In the text that opens this section, the poet identifies himself with an Adam who awakes after a long sleep and is fired by passion. At his side, he finds Eve:

By my side or back of me Eve following,
Or in front, and I following her just the same.[19]

The poem that closes the section, "As Adam Early in the Morning", also portrays an Adam inviting those who surround him to come closer: "Touch me, touch the palm of your hand to my body as I pass,/ Be not afraid of my body". To touch, to feel something with the hand, is a reinvigorating experience for Adam, who in "Song at Sunset" exclaims:

To breathe the air, how delicious!
To speak – to walk – to seize something by the hand!

These lines, which would have continued celebrating the prodigy of naming the living beings, were well known to Pessoa, who had underlined them in his copy of *Leaves of Grass*. Also, for Homeric heroes it was important to introduce themselves, and they did so not by simply pronouncing their names, but rather by singing it in an outburst of enthusiasm and admiration. The true celebration, the supreme exaltation, according to Unamuno, would be to sing

---

[18] In the poem "Ages and ages returning at intervals".
[19] In the poem "To the garden the world".

the name naked and with no frills, and to repeat it constantly, almost immersing one's soul in the ideal content of the word. It is a tendency we find in the poetry of Whitman, characterized by frequent enumerations of names of states, peoples, plants and things. For the Spanish philosopher, when lyrical poetry spiritualizes itself and arrives at the threshold of the sublime, it ends up assuming the shape of mere enumeration (Allen and Folsom 1995: 113).

In 1971, during the award ceremony of the Nobel Prize for Literature, Pablo Neruda justified the excesses and the abundant rhetoric of his work, saying that it was characteristic of American poets to fill with words the confines of a silent continent: "nos embriagaba esta tarea de fabular y de nombrar" ["we were intoxicated by this task of making fables and giving names"]. [20] What Neruda did not mention overtly was the Bible. "American poets" North, however, have been granted, within "the confines of a [hardly] silent continent", a heritage of "making fables and giving names" with a markedly identifying prosody of its own.

What is doubtless is the influence that the Bible exercised on Whitman's versification. In 1933, in an article entitled "Biblical Analogies for Walt Whitman's Prosody", G. W. Allen presented two rhythmic principles in *Leaves of Grass* and pointed out the principal source of inspiration of the work: the Old Testament. The fundamental principles would have been 1) parallelism (repetition of ideas) and 2) anaphor and epanalepsis (repetition of words) (Ferrari 2012). Allen called the former "thought-rhythm" and the latter "phonic-rhythm". Recently, Patricio Ferrari has studied how Caeiro's poetry too is marked by the presence of parallelisms. Probably, the most eloquent example of the rhythmical closeness of *Leaves of Grass* and *O Guardador de Rebanhos* is in the confronting of the second line of "Song of Myself" and a line of poem II of Caeiro's work: "And what I assume you shall assume", "Eu não tenho filosofia: tenho sentidos..." ["I do not have philosophy: I have the senses..."]. Repetition here is not limited to the lexical: Ferrari shows, indeed, how the "phonic-rhythm" is realized too at the level of prosody and structure.

Pessoa was not blind to the strong biblical character of Whitman's work. In the copy he possessed of Perry Bliss's book, *Walt Whitman: His Life and His*

---

[20] Pablo Neruda, "Discurso de Estocolmo".

Work, which he read probably between 1909 and 1910, the Portuguese writer annotated the following passage:

> Ah!
> His own essential model, after all is said, was the rhythmical patterns of the English Bible. Here was precisely that natural stylistic varia-

Detail of p. 96 of *Walt Whitman: His Life and Work*.

Still with respect to rhythm, it is worth noting a comment left by Álvaro de Campos apropos of "ritmo paragráfico" ["paragraphic rhythm"] (Pessoa 1994a: 272). According to the Pessoan heteronym, it was Walt Whitman himself who introduced into poetry the paragraphic rhythm, which was simultaneously an innovation at the level of rhythm and at the level of content. For this reason, it was Campos's opinion that Whitman had been little understood in his day. Whitman's poetry disoriented the reader because it presented inseparably two novelties. Paragraphic rhythm privileged irregular verse, without concern for rhyme, strophe or metre. Rhyme was a cage and poetry tied to rhyme was an artificial poetry:

É-se grande poeta assim? Pode ser-se. Mas é-se grande poeta apesar disto e não por causa disto. É-se grande poeta porque se é grande poeta, e não porque "courage" rima com "rage" ou "son" com "saucisson".

[Is one a great poet thus? One can be. But one is a great poet in spite of this and not because of it. One is a great poet because one is a great poet, and not because "courage" rhymes with "rage" or "son" with "saucisson".]

In this regard, we can refer to poem XIV of the *Guardador de Rebanhos*, the first verses of which are: "Não me importo com as rimas. Raras vezes/ Há duas árvores iguais, uma ao lado da outra" ["I am not concerned with rhymes. Rarely are/ There two trees alike, one beside the other"] (Pessoa 1999: 96). Far from artifice, "o ritmo paragráfico exige uma atenção enorme às ideias, às emoções, à expiração" ["paragraphic rhythm demands an enormous attention to ideas, to emotions, to breathing"] (Pessoa 1999: 273). Campos pursues his reflection, revealing that the same paragraphic rhythm, foreshadowed by William Blake and concretized by Whitman, was also present in his own work and in that of Alberto Caeiro, even if with different hues (because it is different according to its user):

O ritmo paragráfico, quando realmente se obtém, varia com os seus práticos. Largo, complexo, curioso misto de ritmos de verso e de prosa, em Whitman; curto, hirto, dogmático, prosaico sem prosa, poético sem quase poesia, no mestre Caeiro.

[Paragraphic rhythm, when it is really obtained, varies along with its users. A large, complex, curious, mixture of verse and prose rhythms, in Whitman; a short one, prickly, dogmatic, prosaic without prose, poetic almost without poetry, in Master Caeiro.]

Caeiro's disciple, who left his thinking incomplete, pointed to poem XIII of the *Guardador de Rebanhos* as a paradigm of paragraphic rhythm in the work of his Master (Pessoa 1999: 273):

Leve, leve, muito leve,
Um vento muito leve passa,
E vai-se, sempre muito leve.
E eu não sei o que penso
Nem procuro sabê-lo.

[Light, light, very light,
A wind blows very light,
And goes away, ever very light.
And I know not what I think
Nor try to know why.]

Once we have begun to understand the complex network of relationships between Caeiro and Whitman, and between Campos and Whitman (and the way in which Whitman is either present or absent in both), we can, in order fully to appreciate the impact of Whitman on Pessoa's output, see what happens textually when the two heteronyms interact. It is possible, indeed, to notice a parallelism between the manner in which Campos addresses Whitman and that in which Campos addresses Caeiro. In the fragment on "ritmo paragráfico" cited above, the "futurable" heteronym affirmed, "Quem sente deveras não fala em verso, nem mesmo em prosa, mas em grito ou acto" ["Who feels truly does not talk in verse, nor even in prose, but in a shout or an act"] (Pessoa 1994a: 272). A text which can be considered a real *cri de-cœur* is that signed by Campos in 1928, the initial line of which is "Mestre, meu mestre querido!" ["Master, my beloved master!"]. The disciple Campos invokes Caeiro in these terms: "Mestre, meu mestre querido!", "Mestre, meu mestre!", "Meu mestre e meu guia!" ["My master and my guide!"]. Immediately one returns to the section of *Leaves of Grass* entitled "Memories of President Lincoln" and, in particular, to the poem "O Captain! my Captain!". Whitman's poem, written in 1865 and generally classified as an eulogy, was composed in order to honour the sixteenth President of the United States of America, assassinated in that same year. The captain in question was, indeed, Abraham Lincoln, and the ship that had made it through every storm and obtained the final reward was the USA. After the real and metaphorical tempest of the Civil War, the country was – in part – celebrating the end of slavery, but the exultation in the soul of the poet underwent a brusque interruption ("But O heart! heart! heart!") because of the murder of the President, whom Whitman esteemed and considered an ideal guide.

Several readings of "Mestre, meu mestre querido!" in parallel with "Saudação a Walt Whitman" have been suggested. Ramalho is of the opinion that the first thing that strikes the reader of "Mestre, meu mestre querido!" is the anaphoric and contradictory style of Whitman, which also characterized the tribute to the American poet (Santos 2003: 220). Apparently, the way in which Campos addresses Caeiro is comparable with the way he turns to Whitman in the text of 1915. Evident in the verses from 1928, too, is Campos's incapacity to reach the intellectual stature of the other. As a result, a sense of frustration and impotence characterizes entirely "Mestre, meu mestre querido!". The modernist heteronym, aware of the impossibility of identifying himself in his Master, asks him disdainfully:

porque é que ensinaste a clareza da vista,
Se não me podias ensinar a ter a alma com que a ver clara?
[...]
Porque é que me deste a tua alma se eu não sabia que fazer dela [...]?
Porque é que me acordaste para a sensação e a nova alma,
Se eu não saberei sentir, se a minha alma é de sempre a minha?

[why did you teach the clarity of vision,
If you could not teach me to have the soul with which to see it clearly?
[...]
Why did you give me your soul if I did not know what to do with it [...]?
Why did you awaken me to sensation and to the new soul,
If I shall not know how to feel, if my soul is forever mine?]

Caeiro rendered Campos himself and, from that day on, began his disgrace, because – the heteronym affirms – "Eu, por minha desgraça, não sou eu nem outro nem ninguém" ["I, to my disgrace, am not I nor another nor anyone"]. The freedom the Master infused in Campos has become for his disciple a source of anguish:

A calma que tinhas, deste-ma, e foi-me inquietação.
Libertaste-me, mas o destino humano é ser escravo.
Acordaste-me, mas o sentido de ser humano é dormir.

[The calm you had, you gave to me, and it was disquieting.
You released me, but human destiny is to be a slave.
You woke me up, but the meaning of being human is to sleep.]

We recall that, in "Saudação a Walt Whitman", Campos turned to the North American poet, confessing to him:

...hoje, olhando pra trás, só uma ânsia me fica —
Não ter tido a tua calma superior a ti-próprio,
A tua libertação constelada de Noite Infinita.

[...today, looking back, only one anxiety remains —
Not to have had your calm superior to yourself,
Your twinkling liberation of Infinite Night.]

That "calma superior" and that sense of freedom Caeiro and Whitman had in common are for Campos something unattainable. The "versos saltos" ["verse jumps"], "versos pulos" ["verse pulsations"], "versos espasmos" ["verse spasms"], "versos-ataques-histéricos" ["hysteric attack verses"][21] of Campos cannot equal the natural serenity of Caeiro's lines: "Meu mestre, meu coração não aprendeu a tua serenidade./ Meu coração não aprendeu nada./ Meu coração não é nada./ Meu coração está perdido" ["My master, my heart has not learned your serenity./ My heart has not learned anything./ My heart is nothing./ My heart is lost."] (the anaphor recalls the exclamation, "But O heart! heart! heart!" present in "O Captain! my Captain!"). Álvaro de Campos must recognize:

Eu, escravo de tudo como um pó de todos os ventos,
Ergo as mãos para ti, que estás longe, tão longe de mim!

[I, slave of everything as dust of all the winds,
I raise my hands to you, who are far, so far from me!]

A similar distance from his own model was also recognized in the 1915 poem, in which Campos, after asking Whitman when the last train for God would leave, promised him that they would meet at the entrance to the station:

Lá estarei sem o universo, sem a vida, sem eu-próprio, sem nada...
E relembraremos, a sós, silenciosos, com a nossa dor
O grande absurdo do mundo, a dura inépcia das coisas
E sentirei, o mistério sentirei tão longe, tão longe, tão longe,
Tão absoluta e abstractamente longe,
Definitivamente longe.

---

[21] Álvaro de Campos, "Saudação a Walt Whitman".

[I'll be there without universe, without life, without myself, without anything...
And we shall remember, alone, silent, with our pain
The great absurd world, the strong ineptitude of things
And I shall feel, I'll feel the mystery so far, so far, so far,
So absolutely and abstractedly far,
Definitively far.]

Campos does not succeed in matching Caeiro's stature, just as he could not attain to that of Whitman, because Caeiro and Whitman are conceived of as essentially the same thing. It is a theory elaborated by Eduardo Lourenço:

[De resto,] que Caeiro é Walt Whitman em nenhum poema é mais explicitamente confessado, não por Pessoa, mas pela sua linguagem, a mesma com que Walt é saudado. (Lourenço 1973: 127)

[[After all,] no other poem more explicitly confesses that Caeiro is Walt Whitman, not by Pessoa, but by the language of the poem, the same language with which Walt is saluted].

Chapter III
Toings and froings

Did Pessoa mention his mother? She's interesting,
powerful to birth sextuplets
Alberto Caeiro Alvaro de Campos Ricardo Reis
Bernardo Soares & Alexander Search simultaneously
with Fernando Pessoa himself a classic sexophrenic
Allen Ginsberg, "Salutations to Pessoa"

(Frater, peccavi?)
Christian Morgenstern, "Ein Gesang Walt Whitmans"

It is in the light of a notable provocation, again by Susan Margaret Brown, that we proceed:

> Without the model of Whitman, Pessoa might very well have languished and died as a second-rate *fin de siècle* decadent searching in vain for the necessary poetic form to express his fragmented psychic condition. (Brown 1991: 3)

A quick glance at the poetry Pessoa produced before his "encounter" with Whitman furnishes us with some idea about the poet Pessoa might have been. Between 1903 and 1909, during his adolescent years, Pessoa-Search had written a considerable body of poetry in English. In Brown's opinion, the *English Poems* of Alexander Search express a crisis, the crisis of perception of the author's *ego*. It is possible, in fact, to retrace a paralysis in the conception Search had of himself, as well as the attempt to find an "anti-self", an antidote to his acute solipsism. This solipsism derived from the heteronym's incapacity to reconcile his essentially romantic poetic vocation (the desire to explore and express the nature of individual consciousness) with an awareness that such individual consciousness is, in reality, constituted by two irreversibly separated "I"s. The tormented cognition of such an irreconcilability is described in a poem from 1907 entitled "Epitaph". The text is a long epitaph that Search pronounces to commemorate himself, the poet "who thought himself the best/ Of poets in the world's extent" (Pessoa 1995: 100). In the third strophe, we read:

> He lived in powerless egotism,
> His soul tumultuous and disordered
> By thought and feeling's endless schism.

Further on, we discover that the incoherent thoughts and longings of Search had brought him to the brink of madness. We note, too, that the life the young man was leading was cadenced by pain and that he had only enemies (the worst of which was himself):

> He of himself ever did sing,
> Incapable of modesty,
> Lock'd in his wild imagining.

Entrapped in his fervid imagination, though evidently no less caught up in the overt intertextuality – or echo – of "Song of Myself", the early heteronym could not find words to give voice to his inner being:

> His words, though bitter far than hate,
> His bitter soul could not express.

So his fate was to be buried in peace, far removed from other men, from whom, besides, he had always felt apart:

> But let him lie at peace for ever
> Far from the eyes and mouths of men
> And from what him from them did sever.

The epitaph closes by suggesting the idea that thought is a crime that Search has paid for with his life:

He was a thing that God had wrought
And to the sin of having lived
He joined the crime of having thought.

The excised nature of thought is here at the heart of Search's dilemma, one that is also reflected at the level of language. From the *English Poems* there emerges, indeed, a kind of frustration, the consequence of a poetic sensibility confined within conventional canons while needing to explode in freer expressions. A prisoner in such a prospect, Search is stuck in a language he has not created, made up of petrified shapes. It is out of the prison of language that he desperately wants to escape, as we see from the first two strophes of a text of 1904 entitled, simply, "Sonnet":[22]

Could I say what I think, could I express
My every hidden and too silent thought,
And bring my feelings, in perfection wrought,
To one unforced point of living stress;

Could I breathe forth my soul, could I confess
The inmost secrets to my nature brought,
I might be great; yet none to me has taught,
A language well to figure my distress.

Yet day and night to me new whispers bring,
And night and day from me old whispers lake...
Oh for a word, one phrase in which to fling

All that I think or feel and so to wake
The world, but I am dumb and cannot sing –
Dumb as you clouds before the thunders break.

---

[22] This poem was also attributed to the pre-heteronym Charles Robert Anon. Oddly, the word "lake" appears in the original.

Notwithstanding the obvious limitations of the early poems in English (to which, admirably, a not-premature death sentence was proclaimed), they do reveal preoccupations relevant to any consideration of the imminent impact of the discovery of Whitman's writing.

Pessoa and Search, bearing in mind that they were born the same day, at the tender age of sixteen, and rising to the challenge of Arthur Rimbaud's notorious "On n'est pas sérieux, quand on a dix-sept ans" ["One is not serious when one is seventeen"][23], are in search of the words with which to exteriorize what they feel and putatively to shock, thus, the world that surrounds them. Yet the young Search is metaphorically mute and maintains that he is not in a fit state to sing, "dumb as you clouds before the thunders break". If only he could learn a language that would let him express himself, the most intimate secrets of his soul, Search is convinced (alas... and hardly originally) that he would be a great poet.

For Brown, the discovery of this language ("A language well to figure my distress") would not occur until 1910, when Pessoa began to read Walt Whitman. It is relevant to remember that the American poet, in section XXV of "Song of Myself", boasted: "With the twirl of my tongue I encompass worlds and volumes of worlds". What in Walt Whitman attracted Pessoa was ostensibly the capacity of the latter to claim the dual nature of the self and its infinity. As the following lines from "Saudação a Walt Whitman" suggest, it would have been that very multiple, all-encompassing and contradictory person of Whitman who inspired Álvaro de Campos, spurring him on to become a complex cosmos of every emotion, every possibility and every thought:

> Tu, o que eras, tu o que vias, tu o que ouvias,
> O sujeito e o objeto, o ativo e o passivo,
> Aqui e ali, em toda a parte tu,
> Círculo fechando todas as possibilidades de sentir,
> Marco militário de todas as coisas que podem ser,
> Deus Termo de todos os objetos que se imaginem e és tu!

[23] This is the first line of a poem by Arthur Rimbaud from 1870, entitled "Roman".

Tu Hora,
Tu Minuto,
Tu Segundo!
Tu intercalado, liberto, desfraldado, ido,
Intercalamento, libertação, ida, desfraldamento,
Tu intercalador, libertador, desfraldador, remetente,
Carimbo em todas as cartas,
Nome em todos os endereços...

[You, what you were, what you saw, what you heard,
The subject and the object, the active and the passive,
Here and there, everywhere you,
Circle closing every possibility for feeling,
Military measure of all things that there can be,
God Term of all imaginable objects and that is you!
You the Hour,
You the Minute,
You the Second!
You intercalated, liberated, unfurled, gone,
Intercalation, liberation, departure, unfurling,
You intercalator, liberator, unfurler, sender,
Stamp on all the letters,
Name in all the addresses...]

The author of *Leaves of Grass* was an example of how it was possible to be, at one and the same time, subject/object, active/passive, here/there, liberator/liberated. He is like Charles Baudelaire. In a passage of the poem "L'Héautontimorouménos" ["The Man Who Tortures Himself"], he broaches "la vorace Ironie" ["the voracious Irony"] of the poet, or the capacity he possessed for seeing himself doubled, divided into the diverse and opposing parts that constituted him. Thanks to this competence, Baudelaire was aware of being both butcher and victim of himself, knife and plague, slap and cheek:

Je suis le sinistre miroir
Où la mégère se regarde.
Je suis la plaie et le couteau!
Je suis le soufflet et la joue!
Je suis les membres et la roue,
Et la victime et le bourreau!

Je suis de mon coeur le vampire,
– Un de ces grands abandonnés
Au rire éternel condamnés,
Et qui ne peuvent plus sourire! (Baudelaire 1961: 64)

[I am the sinister mirror
In which the shrew looks upon herself.
I am the wound and the dagger!
I am the blow and the cheek!
I am the limbs and the rack,
Victim and executioner!

I am the vampire of my own heart,
– One of those utter derelicts
Condemned to eternal laughter,
But who can no longer smile!]

Alexander Search expressed a typically romantic spiritual exigency, but one no less contested by doubt, by irony and by restlessness; all characteristic, especially, of post-romanticism (Bréchon 1996: 106). The encounter with Whitman permitted Pessoa-Search to overcome the principal problem of his youthful poetry, bypassing at a stroke the dead end in which he had stagnated. According to Brown, it is legitimate to assume that the Portuguese poet had staged the heteronymic *côterie* from 1914 precisely in response to Whitman's exhortation to experiment with a manifold and bulky identity (Brown 1991: 5). Search could therefore be considered "a crisálida de Caeiro, de Reis e de Campos" ["the chrysalis of Caeiro, of Reis and of Campos"] (Bréchon 1996:

105). Most striking is the way in which Pessoa moulded two poetic figures starting from the Whitmanesque formula, "Do I contradict myself?/ Very well then I contradict myself,/ (I am large, I contain multitudes)" in order to embody two aspects of the "I" that are diametrically opposed but inextricably conjoined. In "The Whitman-Pessoa Connection", we read that Whitman had not only offered to Pessoa a new language, but had also furnished him with the blueprints for the creation of two further heteronyms, Alberto Caeiro and Álvaro de Campos. In order more fully to appreciate the subtlety and the complexity of the heteronymic schema, one might analyse just how this dialectic derives from Whitman as a double presence. Both the *totality* of the heteronymic subject (represented by Caeiro) and its *fragmentation* (embodied by Campos) are mutually contradicting personifications of the self. It is arguably the intertextual presence of *Leaves of Grass* that links them, rendering each part inseparable from the other:

> Without the catalyzing force of Whitman, neither Caeiro nor Campos would have been possible. Whitman's mythic, all-encompassing persona offered Pessoa an open-ended epistemology of the self. (Brown 1991: 5)

The poetic figure of Caeiro, therefore, would have emerged in 1914 as a remedy to the deep-seated insecurities of Alexander Search, in particular as a solution to what in "Epitaph" had been defined as the "crime of having thought". It was this "crime" that rendered Search a victim. His own thoughts were consuming him, imprisoning him in obsessive fears and the inability of the young subjectivity to control such panic took him, poem after poem, to the edge of madness. Search's folly sprang from the unconscious confrontation with what in "Horror" (1907) was called "the sense of the mystery of all". The central lines are:

> ... More than all that fear can conceive,
> More than madness can make to believe,
> More than cannot be imagined,
> The sense of the mystery of all,
> When it flashes on me full as can be,

Doth my maddened soul appal.
Speak it not – nor can it be spoken, –
[...]
Think it not, thought is powerless
This horror less than to express. (Pessoa 1995: 118)

The poems of Caeiro resound as a refutation of the problem evoked here. They present, in fact, a strong argument against the validity of thought as a reliable base of knowledge, and negate, thus, the very existence of mystery that had so tormented Search. We emphasized earlier that, in section V of the *Guardador de Rebanhos*, Caeiro affirmed "Há metafísica bastante em não pensar em nada" and "O mistério das coisas? Sei lá o que é mistério!/ O único mistério é haver quem pense no mistério" ["The mystery of things? Who knows what mystery is!/ The only mystery is that there is someone who thinks of mystery"]. A little later, in the same section, there is a probable allusion to such poets as Search:

"Constituição íntima das coisas"...
"Sentido íntimo do Universo"...
Tudo isto é falso, tudo isto não quer dizer nada.
É incrível que se possa pensar em coisas dessas.
É como pensar em razões e fins
Quando o começo da manhã está raiando, e pelos lados das árvores
Um vago ouro lustroso vai perdendo a escuridão.

["The intimate constitution of things"...
"The intimate meaning of the Universe"...
It is all false, it means nothing.
It is incredible that one can think of such things.
It is like thinking of reasons and ends
When the breaking of dawn is aglow, and alongside the trees
A vague golden lustre is losing its darkness.]

Search had never attempted the concrete experience of an immediate look, of an improvised invasion of the self on the part of the spirit of things. In "Horror", he wrote: "such a cowardice of thought/ [...] Takes me, that I fear to open my eyes/ and my mind to a most horrid surprise". In the poem "Thought" (1904), we find: "Thought comes, but blinds the glaring mental sight,/ But shakes our mind with echoes of its roar/ And bears its force beyond our visual scope" (Pessoa 1995: 46). But Caeiro re-establishes the perfect sight of the soul. Both Álvaro de Campos and Ricardo Reis, commenting on the character of the Master, emphasized the importance that the act of seeing had for him. On what was to be the preface to the *Guardador de Rebanhos*, Ricardo Reis wrote:

> Caeiro, no seu objectivismo total, ou, antes, na sua tendência constante para um objectivismo total, é frequentemente mais grego que os próprios gregos [...] Eu era como o cego de nascença, em quem há porém a possibilidade de ver; e o meu conhecimento com *O Guardador de Rebanhos* foi a mão do cirurgião que me abriu, com os olhos, a vista. (Pessoa 1996: 364)

> [Caeiro, in his total objectivism, or better, in his constant tendency to a total objectivism, is often more Greek than the Greeks [...] I was like someone blind at birth, in whom there is nonetheless the possibility of seeing; and my encounter with *O Guardador de Rebanhos* was the surgeon's hand that, through his eyes, opened my sight.]

In similar manner, the disciple Campos confirmed that what he had learned from Caeiro was clear-sightedness:

> O que o mestre Caeiro me ensinou foi a ter clareza; equilíbrio, organismo no delírio e no desvairamento, e também me ensinou a não procurar ter filosofia nenhuma, mas com alma. (Pessoa 1996: 405)

> [What my master Caeiro taught me was to have clarity; balance, organism in delirium and in madness, and he taught me also not to have any philosophy, but with soul.]

The doctrine of seeing was very well known by Walt Whitman, too. Today we know that Pessoa had been in contact with a reflection developed by the author of *Leaves of Grass* that read: "How shall I know what the life is except as I see it in the flesh". The poet of the *drama em gente* had found it in the volume *Walt Whitman: His Life and Work* and had annotated it as important:

> nature with art. There is another troubled entry in one of his early notebooks, which goes to the root of the difficulty: "*How shall my eye separate the beauty of the blossoming buckwheat field from the stalks and heads of tangible matter? How shall I know what the life is except as I see it in the flesh.*"

Walt Whitman: His Life and Work, p. 305.

The sequence of the forty-nine poems of the *Guardador de Rebanhos* appears, thus, like a long declaration of independence of the subject (a "Song of Myself"), an affirmation of his imaginative and transcendental freedom, which probably would not have been possible without the discovery of Whitman. As we anticipated in Chapter I, Pessoa had a copy of *Poems by Walt Whitman* on the introductory lines of which he had annotated "explanation for Caeiro's". It is possible, and it is a hypothesis proposed by Patricio Ferrari, that Pessoa's jotting be understood thus: "explanation for Caeiro's [contradictions]". Whitman would have been so important for the formation of Caeiro that the number of poems destined to be part of the *Guardador de Rebanhos* is also to be considered with regard to the copy of *Poems by Walt Whitman* owned by the Portuguese writer. In a manuscript page, in which the table of contents of the *Guardador de Rebanhos* was planned, Pessoa left this note: "(try to reach 50, or, at the very least, 45) or 49" – namely, close to the number of the sections (51) composing "Song of Myself" in the copy that he had (Ferrari 2011: 45-46).

In what was to be the English preface to a project never brought to conclusion, a collection of *sensacionista* poets, a particularly significant passage is signalled, in which Álvaro de Campos describes himself as follows:

> Álvaro de Campos is excellently defined as a Walt Whitman with a Greek poet inside. He has all the power of intellectual, emotional and physical sensation that characterised Whitman. But he has the precisely opposite trait – a Power of construction and orderly development of a poem that no poet since Milton has attained. (Pessoa 1996: 140)

If Campos is Whitman with a Greek poet inside – and Alberto Caeiro "is often more Greek than the Greeks" – the principal drama of the heteronymic world resides in the implicit dialogue of two incompatible voices within the conscience of Campos: the submissive voice of the all-seeing poet (Caeiro) and the deafening one of the "versos-ataques-histéricos". In the figure of Campos, there would emerge the lacerated awareness of the contingency of existence, an existence bounded by time; therefore, that of the "futurable" heteronym would be an exhausting struggle against time to reappropriate the "calma superior" of Caeiro and Whitman. As observed by Brown:

> Emblematic of the modern poet in a destitute time, Campos searches in vain for traces of the fugitive god, finding nothing but his own dismantled image, his own disbelieving voice. (Brown 1991: 11)

In short, it is her view that it was in response to Whitman's world that Pessoa was able to stage his feelings and his thoughts in a way that, until that moment, he had been incapable of expressing:

> Whitman acted on Pessoa as an incitement to break free, as an invitation to a larger, more spacious geography of the self. (Brown 1991: 2-3)

It was the example of the all-encompassing and contradictory persona of Whitman that armed Pessoa with an instrument to find consolation and a shelter (either *of* or *from* himself) via the strategy of the *drama em gente* [drama in people], and of the *pessoas-livros* [persons-books]. After his seminal contact with Whitman (around 1909-1910), Pessoa has been emptied and filled, destroyed and reassembled. As a consequence, a new Pessoa emerged, a heteronymic Pessoa. However, unlike the North-American poet – who could interweave the wild "barbaric yawp" with the calm "valved voice"[24] – Pessoa had to render himself a modern Whitman, he had to unravel that duality and thus he created Caeiro and Campos.

When it comes to addressing Portuguese literary criticism, it is impossible not to alight on the name of Eduardo Lourenço. His theories are paradigmatically relevant to the aims of this study of the link between Pessoa and Whitman. In *Pessoa Revisitado*, he places the accent on what he judges to be the "prodigious concealment" of Alberto Caeiro's birth. Such an idea arises from the fact that, whilst Pessoa could show with geometric precision the conductor wires that led from Caeiro's universe to Álvaro de Campos and Ricardo Reis, he could not or did not want to explain the apparition of Caeiro in other then miraculous terms (Lourenço 1973: 38). Pessoa saw himself as the creator of Campos and Reis, then, but not of their (and his own) master: it is as if the poetry of the *Guardador de Rebanhos* had rained from on high or had materialized from outside. Pessoa even compared the creation of the heteronyms with the way in which Shakespeare constructed his own characters. Yet, as is emphasized in *Pessoa Revisitado*, Alberto Caeiro is neither the Hamlet nor the Lady Macbeth of Pessoa's literary self, but rather the direct and not recognized manifestation of his own demiurge. At his birth there would be a guilt or a violation that the hyperlucid conscience of his creator rejects, preferring to see himself as created by his own creature. Eduardo Lourenço argues that Pessoa acted in bad faith with regard to the one who came to be defined as the "first" of his heteronyms (first because of the position he occupies in the scenery of his creator, but first in death, too, because Pessoa could not tolerate for more than a moment the weight of a truth that wasn't his own) (Lourenço 1973: 39).

The mystery of the genesis of Caeiro might be unveiled if read in the light of Pessoa's encounter with Whitman. According to Lourenço, although the

---

[24] "Only the lull I like, the hum of your valved voice.", from section V of "Song of Myself".

most immediate connection is that between Whitman and Campos, when one looks more closely at Caeiro, the dominant and essential presence of the latter (not only accidental or decorative) leaps to the attention. From the author of *Leaves of Grass*, Pessoa would have removed the whole skeleton, all appetite and passion for real things, keeping from the violent shock of his reading the scarce nostalgia for a pioneer's strength that was not made for him. Precisely with this yearning would Caeiro be made. The Master, thus, is not Whitman; it is an imaginary and ideal Whitman. This is an opinion shared by Bastos, who, in "Paths Untrodden between Poetry and Philosophy", writes: "Caeiro is contemplative but asexual as if Whitman, depleted of his energy, had been edited by Thoreau" (Bastos (a): 2).

Let us focus instead on the heteronym Álvaro de Campos. As indicated in the letter about the origin of the heteronyms, it was through Campos that Pessoa breathed fresh air, freeing himself (in both a fictitious and a real way) without, however, ceasing to agonize. The Portuguese poet did not have to invent the figure of Campos. He simply met him along his way, as if an open path to the breathing of the world.

Lourenço adds:

[Mas] encontrou-a com o que era e o que era só podia entrar nessa apoplética e cósmica respiração de Walt Whitman *fazendo de conta* que a respirava. (Lourenço 1973: 75)

[[But] he met it being what he was, and what he was could only enter this apoplectic and cosmic breathing of Walt Whitman *bearing in mind* that he was breathing it.]

Indeed, from the very first contact (and not starting from a certain point, as has often been written), Campos adumbrated this breathing from the inside in order to let it become his own, and, always from the inside, he rendered it hysterical. Whitman, on the contrary, has a more ample breath, as we read in section XIV of "Song of Myself":

> I resist any thing better than my own diversity,
> Breathe the air but leave plenty after me,
> And am not stuck up, and am in my place.

One always has the impression, when Campos's poetry hurls itself upon the reader, that the subject is ever in immediate contact with a reality throbbing with feelings, landscapes, lives – a market-place of the world, that is striking in its effervescence, its incessant clamour and in its prodigiousness. Campos would have emerged furiously and all of a sudden exactly to evoke these sensations – not, as had Caeiro, under the cloaked mystery of his impenetrable author (Lourenço 1973: 76). He came out, thus, entire and in good faith from the unconsciously concealed amalgam of Caeiro, who, on the contrary, would be a "glosa e transfigurado eco da visão que Walt Whitman tem das coisas, não do concreto hino com que as canta" ["gloss and transfigured echo of the vision Walt Whitman has of things, not of the concrete hymn through which he celebrates them"] (Lourenço 1973: 78).

The equally impetuous births of Caeiro and Campos would be, according to the author of *Pessoa Revisitado*, symmetrical and would bear witness to the same anxiety and urgency for psychic liberation, but they would outline two inverted figures of a "comedy-drama". Campos's truth would be the overturning of Caeiro's: "ser tudo de todas as maneiras" as a return to that fabulously dispersed Whole that Caeiro had feigned to accept, in his comforting and unmysterious difference, in order to preserve his tranquil and immortal Difference. Only pure multiplicity subsisted for Caeiro; only pure unity was real for Campos. Actually, either the first or the latter lived on what they negated and through that negation they identified in the difference that separated them (Lourenço 1973: 179). Campos could have come to light with his full and false Whitman-like innocence only after Pessoa had proved to himself that he bore within (that he was) an incomparable Master. He proved it through Caeiro. With the references to "being", "value", "meaning" in the poems of the *Guardador de Rebanhos*, Pessoa reached the apex of what, if he were not who he was, would be called simply "megalomania" (Lourenço 1973: 78).

In "Apontamentos para uma estética não-aristotélica" ["Notes towards a non-Aristotelic aesthetics"], Álvaro de Campos (the one who could have turned to Whitman with a filial naturalness and spontaneity) listed what the three key manifestations of non-Aristotelian art were:

A primeira está nos assombrosos poemas de Walt Whitman; a segunda está nos poemas mais que assombrosos do meu mestre Caeiro; a terceira está nas duas odes – a "Ode Triunfal" e a "Ode Marítima" – que publiquei no *Orpheu*. Não pergunto se isto é imodéstia. Afirmo que é verdade. (Pessoa 1980: 251)

[The first one is within the amazing poems of Walt Whitman; the second one resides within the more than amazing poems by my master Caeiro; the third one is within my two odes – "Triumphal Ode" and "Maritime Ode" – that I published in *Orpheu*. I am not wondering if this is immodesty. I affirm it is true.]

That is how Caeiro was placed, voluntarily or involuntarily for other purposes, where he really was, namely, between the "prodigious" poems of Walt Whitman and the admirable odes by Campos. Lourenço is of the view that the entire tragi-comedy of heteronymy ought to be understood in the light of that "ocultação prodigiosa" of Whitman in Caeiro (Lourenço 1973: 80). The issue becomes even more surprising when taking into account that the concealment involved was not as unaware, that is to say unconscious, as at first sight one could suggest, if trusting only in the main documents on the *drama em gente* (that is, the letter to Casais-Monteiro and the "tábua cronológica" ["chronological table"] sent to Côrtes-Rodrigues after the appearance of the heteronyms). According to Lourenço, everything seemed to happen as if Pessoa had not wished publicly to confess to the relationship or the filiation of Caeiro and Whitman. It probably did not suit Pessoa's pride that his first-born should come into the world with the Whitman mask on his face.

Whoever recalls the famous text about the origin of Caeiro, "Escrevi trinta e tantos poemas a fio, numa espécie de êxtase cuja natureza não conseguirei definir" ["I wrote more than thirty poems one after the other, in a kind of ecstasy the nature of which I cannot define"] (Pessoa 1986a: 199), will certainly find some difficulty in reconciling the mysterious birth of Caeiro with the shadow of Whitman hovering over it. The hypothesis advanced by Lourenço is that, whilst the shock Pessoa received from the encounter with Whitman was considerable, no less so was the shock-refusal of this impact. Pessoa enacted, thus, a[n] [un]conscious metamorphosis on the world of Whitman which, one day, came out as similar and "other". This intense process of negation-creation was so consistent as to create in Pessoa the unusual reflex of rooting to the ground the mother text that fascinated him and of inventing Caeiro. This mother text, concealed to the maximum in Caeiro, reappears, however, impeccably in Campos. In consequence, it is fair to say that at the base of the labyrinthine universe of Pessoa "como na memória cega de Édipo, há um *pai*, senão assassinado, integrado sem deixar rasto e em Campos redivivo" ["as in the blind memory of Oedipus, there is a *father*, if not assassinated, still integrated without leaving a trace and revived in Campos"] (Lourenço 1973: 82).

The contradiction between the explanation about the genesis of Caeiro that Pessoa provided and the clear perception of the link unifying Caeiro and Whitman itself points to a disquiet and even a drama in the Pessoan creative consciousness. Indeed, the complex procedure that allowed the pre-heteronymic Pessoa to write Caeiro's poems and then Campos's poems through the double mediation of Walt Whitman is not to be reduced to a simple process of assimilation of the metaphysical (or non-metaphysical) attitude of the singer of *Leaves of Grass*. It would be a matter, rather, of a single movement of fascination and struggle – the attempt carried out by Pessoa to vanquish Whitman on a different level. In this case, Caeiro represents such a checkmating that in it one forgets the adversary, while Campos shows the battle still in play (Lourenço 1973: 83).

The author of *Pessoa Revisitado* throws into relief the "extraordinária psicanálise" ["extraordinary psychoanalysis"] that texts such as "Ode Triunfal", "Ode Marítima" and "Saudação a Walt Whitman" perform and which reveals with a "transparência miraculosa" ["miraculous transparency"] the real bonds that unite the poetry of Whitman with that of Pessoa-Campos (Lourenço 1973: 86). There would be no hint of illusion in the fiction in which Pessoa-Campos believes himself to be another Whitman or at one with him, because nobody knows better than Campos that it is in the *difference* that divides them that his voice – the poetry he is writing – is to be found. In particular, in "Saudação a Walt Whitman", the fact that he finds himself upside down ("Desde Deus vês-me ao contrário") is not a gratuitous pirouette, but rather the genial expression of the relationship between his poetry and the texts of the North American writer. Campos knew that he occupied the space of his exterior imitation, with such precision that he duped himself and us that he really was worthy of Whitman. However, everything turned out as if this external appropriation were a mask of a real inner inadaptability. Through Campos, Pessoa probably confessed to his readers the dimension and the nature of the shock out of which his heteronyms emerged.

Under the sign of Whitman, a euphoric Campos formulated the wish to feel everything in every way, to melt with things to the point of delirium in order to forget about himself, espousing in a single embrace all the contradictions of life. This was his reprise of the old Baudelarian programme to be "la plaie et le couteau/ La victime et le bourreau" and of the Rimbaldian formula on the "dérèglement de tous les sens" ["deregulating of all the senses"],[25] but reinterpreted in terms of a Whitman-Marinetti crusade. The energy imitated in order to sing certain aspects of modern civilization, a melody played by the dexterous hand of Campos – and of direct Whitman derivation – was diminished from the beginning by the ironic accompaniment of the left hand, that is, by the echo of Pessoa's metaphysical fatigue (Lourenço 1973: 177). As a result, and as observed in the texts generally considered as "futurist", the attempt at a magical appropriation of Whitman did not save Campos from himself, "tão contíguo à inércia, tão facilmente cheio de tédio" ["so close to inertia, so easily full of tedium"],[26] and less than ever from his hectic desire to be at one with the world, converted into masochistic and dark passivity

---

[25] "Je veux être poète, et je travaille à me rendre voyant : vous ne comprendrez pas du tout, et je ne saurais presque vous expliquer. Il s'agit d'arriver à l'inconnu par le dérèglement de tous les sens" ["I wish to be a poet, and I work on rendering myself a seer: you will not understand it at all, and I could hardly explain it to you. It is a matter of arriving at the unknown through the deregulation of all the senses"] Rimbaud had written in a letter to Georges Izambard on 13 May 1871.

[26] A line from "Saudação a Walt Whitman".

(Lourenço 1973: 88). We recall that Campos closed "Saudação a Walt Whitman" with the blind conviction of being unable to compete with his Great Liberator. It is possible that this was chronologically the first of the lacerating cries of Campos's creative impotence, at once repeated again and again and in many different ways. Alive in himself and revived in the poems that in their turn *waltwhitmanized* him, Campos is perhaps the most loved Pessoa, the one in whom the greatest number of readers recognize, as if in a fabulously hyperbolic but fraternal mirror, the extraordinary difficulty of existing as they dream (Lourenço 1973: 91).

Eduardo Lourenço argues that the encounter/non-encounter of Pessoa and Whitman is not confined to giving birth to two heteronymic figures from a single creative [im]potency. The enthusiasm of the Portuguese poet in his confronting of the author of *Leaves of Grass* was not exclusively of an aesthetic and literary order. It was, rather, a coming together at a more secret level, the discovery of a hero who celebrated himself as a "Grande Pederasta roçando-[s]e contra a diversidade das coisas" ["Great Pederast rubbing [himself] up against the diversity of things"].[27] Pessoa was well aware that such an example of liberty and self-liberation was inadequate and inaccessible to him and that he would never have imitated it walking in his own shoes. Yet, in its inadequacy, Whitman's example fascinated him. As asserted by Lourenço:

Walt Whitman é o seu Édipo, o que pronunciou a palavra de um enigma análogo ao seu e pronunciando-a o condena literalmente à morte, como Édipo à esfinge. (Lourenço 1973: 95)

[Walt Whitman is his Oedipus, who pronounced the word of an enigma analogous to his own and, pronouncing it, literally condemns him to death, as Oedipus with the Sphinx.]

The enigma in question would have been by nature erotic. In the construction of Campos, singer of free life, democracy and work, Pessoa would have "fixed"

---

[27] A line from "Saudação a Walt Whitman".

(in psychoanalytical terms) on a single point and he would have let gravitate towards it, whether in a literal or in a figurative sense, the important mechanisms of poems such as "Ode Triunfal", "Ode Marítima" and "Saudação a Walt Whitman". This point, as mentioned, was that of erotic passivity, which produced several figures that constantly flowed throughout Campos's poetry, to the extent of an intolerable obsession. Rare in literature are examples of such an open polysemy as that found in "Ode Triunfal" and "Ode Marítima", striking primarily because of its strongly sexual character. What must not be lost from sight is the nature – passive or, more equivocally, active/passive – of the imagery that some passages of the two odes elevate to a monstrously tragic level of self-punishment, always under the sign of a distinctively voluntary excess (Lourenço 1973: 99).

In *Pessoa Revisitado*, Lourenço judges as well founded the hypothesis that the heteronymy can be related to an element of Pessoa's private life: the loss of the father, which occurred when Fernando was five years old. It is possible, according to Lourenço, to assume that the entire spiritual and carnal adventure of the Portuguese writer can be interpreted as an interminable search for the Father. The father figure never appears as such in Pessoa's work (Lourenço 1973: 106). This absence would not arise from indifference or forgetfulness, rather from an intolerable and incurable wound, for the healing of which Pessoa had invented himself little by little. Without a doubt, the absence of the Father constitutes a deep wound. Classically, the infant Pessoa must have loved his father and must have been his unconscious rival. However, fate did not allow him anything else. The death of the man prevented him from solving harmoniously the normal conflict between filial love and jealousy. Nobody gets out from infancy without killing the Father whom one needs in order to become an adult. Yet, Pessoa did not have this opportunity. He had, instead, the tremendous pressure of assuming the role of his disappeared father, to be in a certain sense "a little father of himself". As Lourenço sustains: "A ausência do pai desfalcou-o do super-ego de que necessitava para afirmar o seu" ["The absence of the father deprived him of the super-ego which he needed to affirm his self"] (Lourenço 1973: 108). This fact had a double consequence: it eliminated Pessoa's capacity to identify with the paternal model and deprived him of the object of the unconscious rivalry of the infant Pessoa.

In a letter to João Gaspar Simões of 11 December 1931, Pessoa criticized Freudianism ("É estreito se julgamos, por ele, que tudo se reduz à sexualidade, pois nada se reduz a uma coisa só" ["It is narrow if we are to judge, by that, that everything is reducible to sexuality, since nothing can be reduced to but one thing alone"]) and, in particular, the reductive character of the critical methodology inspired by psychoanalysis (Pessoa 1980: 175). What he refused (and from which he defended himself with a sincere panic) was the risk of being "interpreted" in the light of Freudian theories. Those new theories permitted that absolutely obscene books were written for scientific purposes and that present and past artists and writers were interpreted (generally without any critical base at all) in a very degrading gossipy way. Nevertheless, Pessoa could grant to Freud certain merits, one of which was that of focusing the attention of doctors on an important element of the "vida da alma" ["life of the soul"]: "a sexualidade, cuja importância havia sido, por diversos motivos, diminuída ou desconhecida anteriormente" ["sexuality, whose importance had been diminished or denied before for several reasons"] (Pessoa 1980: 175). About this topic, however, Pessoa did not speak in his letter to Gaspar Simões:

> dado o pouco que sempre me interessou a sexualidade, própria ou alheia – a primeira pela pouca importância que sempre dei a mim mesmo, como ente físico e social, a segunda por um melindre (adentro da minha própria cabeça) de me intrometer, ainda que interpretativamente, na vida dos outros. (Pessoa 1980: 175)

> [given how little that sexuality, my own and others', always interested me – the first one because of the scarce importance I have always given to myself as a physical and social entity, the second one because of a scruple (in my head) of interfering in the life of other people, even if interpretatively.]

A "British" prudishness in the Portuguese poet was known among his friends, because one day one of them warned the others not to say indecencies in Pessoa's presence. In fact, in a page of Pessoa's diary dated 8 March 1913, one reads this annotation:

> Frases casuais, nem sequer comigo (excepto, o que, felizmente, aguentei risonho e calmo, a citação pelo Almada das frases – pedido que o Castañé lhe fez, de que não dissessem indecências diante de mim) (Pessoa 1996: 32)

> [Accidental phrases, not even with me (except what, fortunately, I tolerated cheerfully and calmly, the quoting of phrases of Almada – request made by Castañé, of not saying indecencies in my presence)]

It is impossible not to catch sight of a contradiction between the cold virginity of his real life and the erotic overflowing of poems such as "Ode Marítima". It seems that one cannot reconcile Álvaro de Campos with the angelic, an archetype of his creator (an archetype also represented by Alberto Caeiro, the ideally absent sex that does not comprehend either a feminine or a masculine presence) (Lourenço 1973: 118). Still, Lourenço suggests as conceivable a natural agreement between the two sides. He considers that Pessoa might occupy, erotically speaking, a space somewhere between Baudelaire and Proust, namely, a space of rejection, which is double and opposite to that which was granted to the former and to the latter. It would not, therefore, be a matter of indifference to sex or a real and actual impotence, rather a desperate and double struggle to suffocate the expression of an Eros considered to be outside the common norm and transform it into a "normalized" Eros. One finds traces of this battle in a reflection written by Pessoa about the nature of his impulses:

> Não encontro dificuldade em definir-me: sou um temperamento feminino com uma inteligência masculina. A minha sensibilidade e os movimentos que dela procedem, e é nisso que consistem o temperamento e a sua expressão, são de mulher. As minhas faculdades de relação – a inteligência, e a vontade, que é a inteligência do impulso – são de homem. (Pessoa 1996: 27)

[I find no difficulties in describing me: I am a feminine temperament with a masculine intelligence. My sensibility and the movements that from it proceed, and it is of this that the temperament and its expression consist, are those of a woman. My faculties of connection – intelligence and will, which is the intelligence of impulse – are those of a man.]

The poet continues the self-analysis, explaining that he always preferred being loved to loving someone, and that he privileges passivity:

Agradava-me a passividade. De actividade, só me aprazia o bastante para estimular, para não deixar esquecer-me, a actividade em amar daquele que me amava. (Pessoa 1996: 27)

[I liked passivity. Of activity, I liked only enough to stimulate, enough not to let them forget me, the loving activity of the one who loved me.]

Pessoa, then, recognized the nature of this phenomenon: it was a frustrated sexual inversion. Though limited to the spirit, the poet always felt troubled by the possibility that this tendency of temperament could reach the body. The fear that this spiritual inversion might be translated onto the physical level derived from his observation of how Shakespeare and Rousseau had realized it: the first with pederasty, and the second with a vague masochism. Despite the presence of several personalities with this inclination in the artistic world, Pessoa affirmed that he would have felt humiliated to death if he had felt the desire to perform the sexuality corresponding with his impulses.

It is a broadly shared view that Christian culture in the west is a culture of blame and that sex has to suffer, from the beginning, the weight of a guilt. Plunged into this kind of culture, Pessoa is presumed to have blamed himself for the sexual impulses he felt and, at the same time, despised himself because he could neither accept them nor translate them to the plane of a "normal" Eros. In *Pessoa Revisitado*, the suggestion is made for the whole work of Pessoa to be read as being the painful labyrinth of this ambiguity that struggled through every means to get out from itself (Lourenço 1973: 145). The only key Eros possessed to liberate itself was that of Poetry, and it found a spectacular and tragic expression in heteronymy. At the base of Campos, as at the base of Caeiro, Reis and Pessoa, would shine the dark light of an intimate secret contaminating everything with its shadow. This would be the mirror of a conscience fragmented into a thousand pieces by the sense of guilt.

Lourenço stresses, however, how Pessoa would never have shaped his heteronymic *côterie* without the mediation of other poetic universes. What can appear to be a common tendency assumed, in the author of *Fausto* [*Faust*] and *O Marinheiro* [*The Mariner*], an extraordinary form. Worthy of Shakespeare, Pessoa's behaviour was very similar to that of Hamlet, who made use of a play within a play in order to produce to his own eyes, and to others', "the truth" he was not as yet able to admit (Lourenço 1973: 146-7).

The attitude of the poet Pessoa in his 'twenties was one of competitiveness and rivalry towards those who had left a footprint on the path he was taking. This was how the young man regarded not only Whitman, but also Shakespeare, Goethe and Symbolism (Lourenço 1973: 148). This conduct led to different results not because Pessoa was different, but because each of the literary encounters he made put to him new questions and demanded from him always more complex answers. Unlike Brown, who situates it between 1909 and 1910, Lourenço believes that the encounter between Pessoa and Whitman had occurred around 1914. He reiterates that this was not an encounter like those Pessoa had annotated in his "Tábua Bibliográfica", but rather an authentic trauma, the "violation" of the inner domicile of the Portuguese poet. Just as Pessoa was the poet predestined by the depression of the European soul, and in particular of the Portuguese one, Whitman was the poet of difference, of the exaltation of the individual in his divine singularity. From the encounter, the collision, with this tumultuous vision the heteronyms sprang up. According to Lourenço, from the author of *Leaves of Grass* Pessoa had learned the poetics of Difference as sign of the real, adding only his specific masochist touch (Lourenço 1993: 17).

Revisiting the nature of the encounter of Pessoa with Whitman, Richard Zenith starts from Lourenço's observations, adding to them some information that has emerged only very recently. Zenith opines that not only Álvaro de Campos but also Alberto Caeiro is characterized by passivity, in contrast with the propensity and concrete life of Whitman, who really wandered through the fields, taking maximum advantage of urban reality, dirtying his hands and rubbing his body against others. In contrast, the core of the two heteronyms would be an essential unhappiness, a lacerated conscience. Awareness was for Whitman a source of joy because it increased the author's pleasure in tasting and smelling the things that surrounded him, seeing and touching them. In section XXV of "Song of Myself", we read: "My knowledge my live parts, it keeping tally with the meaning of all things,/ Happiness (which whoever hears me let him or her set out in search of this day)". For Pessoa, in every heteronymic corner of his personality, consciousness implied suffering. Happiness, wherever it was, resided in unawareness, in ignorance and in forgetfulness. Thinking, being aware of his own existence, was for the creator of the *pessoas-livros*, a sort of malediction. Interiority presupposes a split from ignorance and unconsciousness and an introduction into the abyss of being. Whosoever goes through this kind of initiation can never go back to pure exteriority – thus, the loss of innocence and the withering of the spirit caused by analyzing everything and searching for a supreme nakedness (Coelho 1971: 98).

As Unamuno affirmed in 1912, "El hombre, por ser hombre, por tener conciencia, es ya, respecto al burro o a un cangrejo, un animal enfermo. La conciencia es una enfermedad" ["Man, for being man, is already, unlike the donkey or the crab, a sick animal. Conscience is an illness"] (Unamuno 1995: 34). This very infirmity was staged in *Fausto*, the "subjective" tragedy on which Pessoa worked at various times but did not manage to bring to a conclusion. Fausto came to the point of envying the unconsciousness of the "others", of all those who were not him. We may take as an example a passage from act IV:

> Desde que despertei para a consciência
> Do abismo da morte que me cerca,
> Não mais ri nem chorei, porque passei,
> Na monstruosidade do sofrer,
> Muito além da loucura da que ri
> Ou da que chora, monstruosamente
> Consciente de tudo e da consciência
> Que de tudo horrivelmente tenho. (Pessoa 2013: 181)

[Since I woke up to the awareness
Of the abyss of death that surrounds me,
I have never laughed nor cried, because I passed,
Throughout the monstrosity of suffering,
Far beyond the laughing
Or the crying madness, monstrously
Conscious of everything and of the awareness
That I have of everything.]

This envy of others' lack of awareness recurs in numerous poems by the orthonym Pessoa and probably finds its highest expression in a text from 1924, "Ela canta, pobre ceifeira":

Ah, poder ser tu, sendo eu!
Ter a tua alegre inconsciência,
E a consciência disso! (Pessoa 2009: 361)

[Oh, to be you, being me!
To have your joyful unconsciousness,
And the consciousness of it!]

In the heteronym Campos, such a condition of hyper-lucidity became a poetical matter, whilst Caeiro would seem to have provided the only moment of calm in Pessoa's created world – *Mestre* Caeiro is considered by Leyla Perrone-Moisés and Richard Zenith to be the "Zen" heteronym of the Pessoan galaxy, but his tranquility is probably just a consolation prize, the peace derived from detachment and resignation (Zenith 2013: 41).

It is hardly surprising that the hyper-conscious Pessoa had already anticipated in respect of his own writings many of the observations later to be put forward by Lourenço. In some unpublished manuscripts, or those published only recently, the poet confirms certain of the interpretations intuitively formulated by the Portuguese critic. In a prose text first published a few years ago, for example, Pessoa seemed to agree with the hypothesis expressed in *Pessoa Revisitado* about the origin of Caeiro, that is "A Whitman,

Pessoa tirou todos os ossos, todo o apetite e a paixão das coisas reais" ["Pessoa took off from Whitman all the bones, all the appetite and the passion for real things"] (Lourenço 1973: 46-7). This portrait leads one to believe that the keeper of flocks was a reduced and impoverished version of Whitman, but the comparative analysis of the two poets performed by Pessoa affirmed the exact contrary. Handwritten in English, this analysis announced from the first line ("Differences between Whitman and Caeiro are clear") the contrasting nature of the comparison. We cite in its entirety the text elaborated by Pessoa, just as it has been deciphered and transcribed by Zenith in "Pessoa and Walt Whitman Revisited":

> Differences between Whitman and Caeiro are clear:
> - Caeiro is clear. Whitman is confused, muddled.
> - Caeiro is a subtler rhythmist thanWhitman.
> - Caeiro is far more of an intellectual than Whitman.
> - We are convinced there is no influence at all. Caeiro is so like and so different from Whitman, he is so near and so far from him, that if he knew him he would [n]either come nearer [n]or go farther away.
> - Whitman rarely has the tender emotion that is constantly characteristic of Caeiro. Caeiro is an atheist St Francis of Assisi. Whitman can neither be called an atheist nor a St Francis of Assisi.
> - Whitman has nothing like Caeiro's 8th and _th and _th poems.
> - Caeiro is a greater purely lyrical poet than Whitman. Whether himself active or not, Whitman is a poet of action. Caeiro is a purely contemplative poet. Caeiro is ever abstract, even when he is concrete. It has been noted – how different from Whitman! – that he never names a particular tree or flower. He only speaks of trees and flowers in the absolute abstract.
> - Even when their attitudes seem [a]like, Whitman is always clearly democratic. Caeiro's not obtrusively but very clearly and very evidently aristocratic.
> Man [–] Whitman – Caeiro seems a natural evolution.
> Swinburne has spoken truest of Whitman: "Never before was high poetry so puddled and adulterated with mere doctrine in its crudest form." Though Caeiro's poetry is almost all mere doctrine, it cannot be said of it that it in any ways puddles and adulterates the undeniable poetry. It is

poetry and philosophy simultaneously and interpenetratedly. We read Caeiro's poetry and know that in no notebook of his (if he keeps notebooks) could we find anything like Whitman's "Get from Mr Arkhurst the names of all insects – interweave a train of thought suitable." He is both too concrete to obtain his concrete facts thus second-hand, and too abstract to care for the facts thus [obtained]. The swing of his pendulum is greater than Whitman's. It is more concrete and more abstract, more materialistic and more spiritualistic, both clearer and more complex.
Caeiro, besides, is essentially disciplined.
Their fundamental standpoints, after all, have only one thing in common – the opposition to civilization, to convention and to pure thoughts, qua pure thoughts.
All the rest is different. Caeiro is a radical enemy of all creeds; his creed, which is none at all, sets them all aside. Whitman's includes all. And this is ample proof of Caeiro's eminently intellectual attitude. He sees clearly and logically. A creed including all creeds, if greater, is also vaguer than them all. (Zenith 2013: 49-50)

The first four points of Pessoa's list are particularly resonant and, in all probability, are an indicator of the anxiety felt by the poet masked as a critic.The emphatic fourth point in particular, "We are convinced there is no influence at all", obviously persuades us of the contrary, that Whitman's influence upon Caeiro has indeed been considerable. After a list of other dissimilarities, we read of Caeiro's supremacy as a "pure" lyrical poet: unlike the author of *Leaves of Grass*, the keeper of flocks is an essentially contemplative poet, abstract even when he is concrete. It is under the sign of this absolute abstractness that he speaks about trees and flowers, without ever mentioning the proper name of any species. Thus, Pessoa was not only aware of the abstract way in which Caeiro looked at the world: he thought that such an attitude situated the Master in a renowned position compared to Whitman, who was always interested in the particular. Later, in the analysis carried out by Pessoa, it is explained, in fact, that in no notebook belonging to Caeiro could one chance upon an annotation like the one left by Whitman: "Get from Mr Arkhurst the names of all insects – interweave a train of thought suitable". Confirmation of such an inclination of Caeiro is to be found in "Notas Para a

Recordação do Meu Mestre Caeiro", drafted by Álvaro de Campos around 1931. Here, Campos evokes a conversation held some time before with his mentor. Wanting to translate into Portuguese some verses by Wordsworth, but without knowing the equivalent of the English term "primrose", Campos defined the primrose as a generic "flor amarela" ["yellow flower"] (Pessoa 1999: 266). Wordsworth's lines "A primrose by the river's brim/ A yellow primrose was to him,/ And it was nothing more" were translated into Portuguese thus: "Uma flor à margem do rio/ Para ele era uma flor amarela,/ E não era mais nada". Campos reports that Caeiro initially agreed with the attitude of the lyrical subject:

> Esse simples via bem: uma flor amarela não é realmente senão uma flor amarela. (Pessoa 1999: 266)

> [That simplicity worked well: a yellow flower is really nothing other than a yellow flower.]

However, after thinking a little, he corrected himself:

> Há uma diferença [...] Depende se se considera a flor amarela como uma das várias flores amarelas, ou como aquela flor amarela só [...] O que esse seu poeta inglês queria dizer era que para o tal homem essa flor amarela era uma experiência vulgar, ou uma coisa conhecida. Ora isso é que não está bem. Toda a coisa que vemos, devemos vê-la sempre pela primeira vez, porque realmente é a primeira vez que a vemos. E então cada flor amarela é uma nova flor amarela, ainda que seja o que se chama a mesma de ontem. A gente não é já o mesmo nem a flor a mesma. O próprio amarelo não pode ser já o mesmo. (Pessoa 1999: 268)

> [There is one difference [...] It depends whether one considers the yellow flower as one of the many yellow flowers, or as that yellow flower only [...] What this English poet of yours wanted to say is that for that specific man that yellow flower was an everyday experience, or something known. Now that is what is not right. Everything we see, we ought to see it always for the first time, because it really is the first time that we see it. And so, each

yellow flower is a new yellow flower, even though it is called the same as yesterday. People are not the same, and the flower is not the same. Yellow itself can no longer be the same.]

It was a pity, for Caeiro, that human beings were not up to grasping this simple concept. If they had done so, everyone would have been happy.

In the lines of *Leaves of Grass*, on the contrary, one notices the presence of a specific terminology referring to the natural elements. In "Song of Myself" alone, elder, mullein, hellebore and morning glories are mentioned. If one is curious to know how Pessoa might have read the annotation left by Whitman in his own notepad ("Get from Mr Arkhurst the names of all insects – interweave a train of thought suitable"), it is sufficient to glance at the copy of *Walt Whitman: His Life And Work* owned by the Portuguese poet, on which Pessoa left the following comment.

> AFTER FIFTY YEARS 305
>
> it is not only imagination, but even thought that is lacking. "Get from Mr. Arkhurst the names of all insects — interweave a train of thought suitable," is Whitman's notebook formula for composing a proposed poem; but on page after

Walt Whitman: His Life and Work, p. 305.

Turning to the contrastive analysis formulated by Pessoa, we read: "Whitman is always clearly democratic. Caeiro's not obtrusively but very clearly and very evidently aristocratic." That the American poet had a more democratic disposition than the author of the *Guardador de Rebanhos* is indubitable. Let us focus, for example, on this passage from section XVI of "Song of Myself":

Of every hue and caste am I, of every rank and religion,
A farmer, mechanic, artist, gentleman, sailor, quaker,
Prisoner, fancy-man, rowdy, lawyer, physician, priest.
I resist any thing better than my own diversity...

For Whitman, both orality and writing were democratic; on the contrary, Pessoa was of the view that writing was always aristocratic: "A linguagem falada é popular. A linguagem escrita é aristocrática" ["Spoken language is popular. Written language is aristocratic"] (Pessoa 1993b: 112). As observed by Bastos:

> Whitman could not have written, as Pessoa did, that writing was aristocratic. For him both were democratic, and speech would be placed naturally before writing, until they got entangled in one entity, like poetry and philosophy. (Bastos (a): 8)

In the last point of the list compiled by the creator of the heteronyms, it is asserted that, despite Whitman and Caeiro having one thing in common (the opposition to civilization), everything else diverges. In particular, Caeiro is against all doctrines and excludes all creeds; by contrast, Whitman welcomes every faith, and this behaviour is judged by Pessoa thus: "A creed including all creeds, if greater, is also vaguer than them all". It was Whitman himself who in "Song of Myself" affirmed:

> My faith is the greatest of faiths and the least of faiths,
> Enclosing worship ancient and modern and all between ancient and modern,
> Believing I shall come again upon the earth after five thousand years,
> Waiting responses from oracles, honoring the gods, saluting the sun,
> Making a fetich of the first rock or stump, powowing with sticks in the circle of obis,
> Helping the llama or brahmin as he trims the lamps of the idols,
> [...] to Shastas and Vedas admirant, minding the Koran,
> [...] accepting the Gospels, accepting him that was crucified, knowing assuredly that he is divine...

Among all the observations made by Pessoa, there is a curious note that, however, he did not develop: "Man [–] Whitman – Caeiro seems a natural evolution". It is Zenith's opinion that one can read this transformation in historical terms: the abstract and incorporeal Caeiro would be an updated Whitman, a Whitman of the twentieth century (Zenith 2013: 43). In the eyes of Pessoa, Whitman probably needed a renewal because his American optimism, his democratic idealism and his appeal to universal brotherhood were too innocent a concept, of which the disenchanted modern individual could no longer avail himself. In an epoch in which life was marked by accelerated rhythms, Whitman's attention to the concrete detail was losing importance. Poetry, by continuing to be stimulating, ought to arrive more quickly at the core of the subject dealt with. In all probability, Pessoa perceived the "virtual" direction that literature was taking.

In "Pessoa and Walt Whitman Revisited", at a certain point, Zenith distances himself from the theories elaborated by Lourenço. In fact, whilst the Portuguese critic supposed that Pessoa had discovered Whitman between 1913 and 1914 (and, at the time, there were no proofs to belie it), Zenith could demonstrate that the encounter between the two had occurred much earlier, probably in 1906-1907. In one of Pessoa's notebooks, among reflections upon the origin of idealism, one finds this comment, written in English and dating back to 1907-1908:

> Walt Whitman united all 3 tendencies, because he united mania of doubt, exaltation of personality, and euphory of physical "ego". (Zenith 2013: 45)

It is at least six years before the appearance of Caeiro, Campos and Reis, and the North American poet had already joined the cauldron of readings fermenting inside the young Pessoa. Zenith refutes, thus, the hypothesis of the filial link, which would have united Caeiro and Campos with Whitman:

> To say that Caeiro and Campos were born of Whitman, whom they proceed to subvert, is to draw a long and implausibly narrow line. (Zenith 2013: 45)

Such a position is shared by Ramalho, who restates:

> To say that the Pessoan affiliative heteronyms originate in the Portuguese poet's proper reading of *Leaves of Grass* may be to make too much ado about Whitman. (Santos 2003: 70)

Toings and froings

Apart from evincing circumspection regarding the dangers of an over-Freudian take on the ostensible Whitman legacy, such alternative readings open, again, other avenues of speculation.

The heteronyms would have been born out of an amalgam of influences that for *Mestre* Caeiro would include Teixeira de Pascoaes, Cesário Verde, Guerra Junqueiro, Francis Jammes, and Alice Meynell; while for Campos they would include Nietzsche, Cesário Verde, the futurists and Oscar Wilde. We find extremely relevant the fact that Caeiro wanted to transmit of himself the image of the illiterate poet, while it is evident that he had received a literary formation. In the preface to the *Guardador de Rebanhos*, Ricardo Reis wrote:

> Ignorante da vida e quase ignorante das letras, [...] fez Caeiro a sua obra por um progresso imperceptível e profundo... (Pessoa 1999: 28)

> [Ignorant of life and almost ignorant of literature, [...] Caeiro produced his work through an imperceptible and deep progress...]

In section XII of the *Guardador de Rebanhos*, the selfsame Caeiro affirmed:

> Os pastores de Virgílio tocavam avenas e outras coisas
> E cantavam de amor literariamente.
> (Depois – eu nunca li Virgílio.
> Para que o havia eu de ler?) (Pessoa 1999: 90)

> [Vergil's shepherds played the reed and other things
> And sang literarily about love.
> (Then – I have never read Vergil.
> Why would I have to read him?)]

Soon after, in poem XXVIII, Caeiro tells how the reading of a mystic poet (clearly Teixeira de Pascoaes) made him laugh:

> Li hoje quase duas páginas
> Do livro dum poeta místico,
> E ri como quem tem chorado muito.

Os poetas místicos são filósofos doentes,
E os filósofos doentes são homens doidos. (Pessoa 1999: 122)

[Today I read almost two pages
Of the book of a mystic poet,
And I laughed like one who has cried a lot.

Mystical poets are ill philosophers,
And ill philosophers are mad men.]

Yet, as we read in the preface, the entire collection of the *Guardador de Rebanhos* was dedicated to Cesário Verde: "Esta obra inteira é dedicada por desejo do próprio autor à memória de Cesário Verde" ["This entire work is dedicated, by the author's will, to the memory of Cesário Verde"] (Pessoa 1999: 32). A similar contradiction is traceable in the so-called "semi-heteronym" Bernardo Soares who, in the preface of the *Livro do Desassossego* [*Book of Disquiet*], is described as a man who takes no pleasure in reading.[28] Soares confirmed: "Não posso ler, porque a minha crítica hiperacesa não descortina senão defeitos, imperfeições e possibilidades de melhor" ["I can't read, because my hyper-alert criticism uncovers only defects, imperfections and possibilities for something better"] (Pessoa 1982: 191). This declaration, however, is completely reversed in the following pages, as only in the first half of the *Livro do Desassossego* does one find references to Cesário Verde, Shakespeare, António Vieira, Lamartine, Horace, Machiavelli, Kant, Goethe,

---

[28] In the letter of 13 January 1935 to Adolfo Casais Monteiro that we have already mentioned, Fernando Pessoa describes thus the concept of semi-heteronymy: "O meu semi-heterónimo Bernardo Soares [...] aparece sempre que estou cansado ou sonolento, de sorte que tenha um pouco suspensas as qualidades de raciocínio e de inibição; aquela prosa é um constante devaneio. É um semi-heterónimo porque, não sendo a personalidade a minha, é, não diferente da minha, mas uma simples mutilação dela. Sou eu menos o raciocínio e a afectividade" ["My semi-heteronym Bernardo Soares [...] always appears when I am tired or drowsy and, as a consequence, his qualities of reasoning and inhibition are a little suspended; his prose is a constant daydream. He is a semi-heteronym because his personality, without being mine, is a simple mutilation of mine. It is me, minus ratiocination and affection"].

Shelley, Dickens, Mallarmé, Verlaine, Carlyle, Rousseau, Hegel, Pessanha, Chateaubriand, Hugo etc. (Castro 2016: 204). A similar posture can be found in Whitman:

> Numa recensão do seu livro apensa a *Folhas de Erva*, Walt Whitman pretende que nunca frequentou homens de letras, nem leu nada. Exatamente como Caeiro evocado por Álvaro de Campos. (Ferrari 2011: 44)[29]

> [In a review attached to *Leaves of Grass*, Walt Whitman claims he never frequented men of letters, nor read anything. Exactly like the Caeiro evoked by Álvaro de Campos.]

We know that Whitman adored a photograph of him taken by W. Curtis Taylor in 1877, to the point of wanting it reproduced as frontispiece to his 1891 edition of *Leaves of Grass*. The photo, which would serve to promote the image of the poet as uncontaminated by civilization and, rather, as a man wholly at one with Nature, portrayed Whitman with a butterfly resting on his right hand. According to the author, he and lepidoptera were good friends – in fact, quite visibly, there is a thread around Whitman's finger that ties it to the fake butterfly.

The theme of the butterfly had already appeared in the 1860 edition of *Leaves of Grass*. The collection – which was distributed with various covers in differently coloured materials – was interspersed throughout with illustrations of butterflies, globes and suns. The volume of *Imprints* of 1860 showed the drawing of a butterfly sitting on a finger of the right hand.

It will certainly have been such indissociable imagery that explains Federico García Lorca's reference in the ode that he dedicated to Walt Whitman:

> Ni un solo momento, viejo hermoso Walt Whitman,
> he dejado de ver tu barba llena de mariposas...

---

[29] Ferrari refers the reader here to an affirmation of Eduardo Lourenço, in "Walt Whitman e Pessoa", in *Poesia e Metafísica*. Lisboa: Sá da Costa, 1983.

[Not for one moment, lovely old Walt Whitman,
Have I stopped seeing your beard full of butterflies...]

Also in the work of Alberto Caeiro, the presence of the insect is relevant. In poem XL of the *Guardador de Rebanhos*, we read:

Passa uma borboleta por diante de mim
E pela primeira vez no Universo eu reparo
Que as borboletas não têm cor nem movimento,
Assim como as flores não têm perfume nem cor.
A cor é que tem cor nas asas da borboleta,
No movimento da borboleta o movimento é que se move.
O perfume é que tem perfume no perfume da flor.
A borboleta é apenas borboleta
E a flor é apenas flor.

[A butterfly passes before me
And for the first time in the Universe I notice
That butterflies have neither colour nor movement,
Just as flowers have neither perfume nor colour.
It is colour that has colour on the wings of the butterfly,
In the movement of the butterfly, it is the movement that moves.
Perfume is what is perfume in the perfume of the flower.
The butterfly is just a butterfly
And the flower is just a flower.]

The ascendency of Whitman in Pessoa's work is retraceable not only in the poetry of the heteronyms but also in the writings of the mature Pessoa and in his own person. According to Zenith, one can consider Whitman as a catalyst, an ingredient stirred into the Pessoan mix around 1907, but the reaction of which on the other elements that had contributed to the intellectual formation of Pessoa was manifested more intensely in 1913 or in 1914. As stated by Brown, Whitman had liberated the Portuguese poet *from* himself and *to* himself. What freed Pessoa from himself would have been the audacity and the impudence of the author of *Leaves of Grass* in singing his own subjectivity without limits and without excuses (Zenith 2013: 45).

Whitman with butterfly, 1877, W. Curtis Taylor (Broadbent & Taylor)

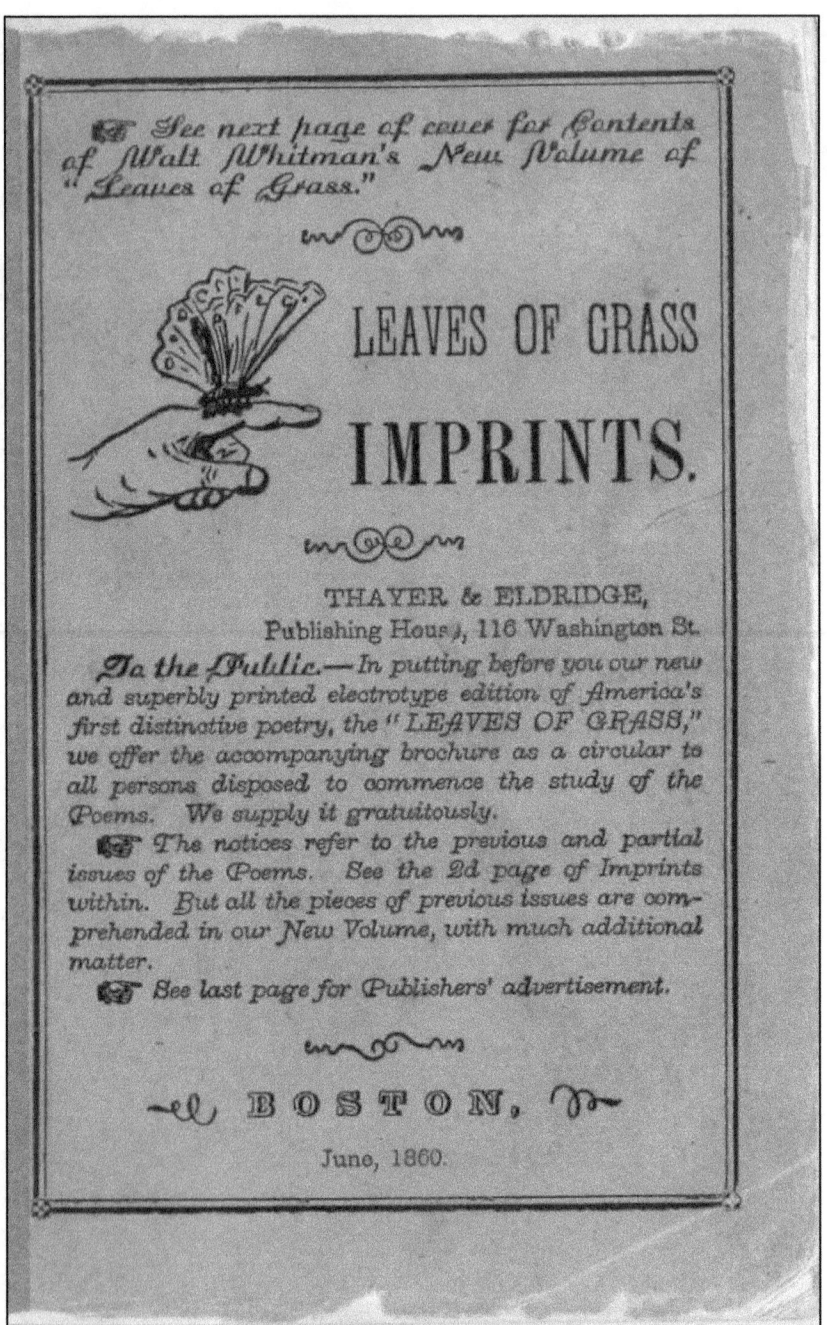

Leaves of Grass. Imprints, 1860.

Through the formula "Do I contradict myself?/ Very well then I contradict myself/ (I am large, I contain multitudes)", Whitman did not teach Pessoa to contradict and to contain diverse personalities. He simply freed him to become what he already was. Still, Pessoa, in a certain sense, would have taken the North American poet as a model to imitate or to embody. This would be the way in which Whitman helped Pessoa to be freed from himself. Specifically, it is possible to talk about manipulation, exploitation and even rape. Pessoa has been possessed by Whitman, or by the image that Whitman had bequeathed to posterity, and has adapted him to his own persona/personae and to his own project: "It is this Pessoanised Whitman that can be considered, with some justice, a heteronymic brother, exactly as Campos describes him in 'Saudação'" (Zenith 2013: 46).

In a fragment on the "ritmo paragráfico" cited earlier, we find an explicit confession, which shows that Pessoa has consciously produced a Portuguese version of Whitman for domestic use, at a time when nothing of the kind had yet been done in Portugal (Pessoa 1994a: 272). Here, Campos, after affirming that Whitman had been the first to possess a "sensibilidade futurista", declared that the same effect of "ahurissement" ["bewilderment"], of disorientation, of Whitman's poetry had also been provoked by "Ode Triunfal":

O mesmo *ahurissement* produzi eu com a minha "Ode Triunfal", no *Orpheu 1*, visto que, embora escrita perto de setenta anos depois da primeira edição das *Leaves of Grass*, aqui ninguém sabia sequer da existência de Whitman, como não sabem em geral da própria existência das coisas. (Pessoa 1994a: 272)

[I produced the same *ahurissement* with my "Triumphal Ode", in *Orpheu 1*, because, even though it was written almost seventy years after the first edition of *Leaves of Grass*, here nobody even knew about the existence of Whitman, just as they do not know, generally speaking, about the very existence of things.]

It is Zenith's opinion that the "true" Whitman, the one that Pessoa had not wished to appropriate, had used the imagination in order to be in contact with the real world. On the contrary, Pessoa had lived through the imagination because the real world was too small and imperfect. The North American writer wanted to feel, and apparently felt, that he was an integral part of humanity. The creator of the heteronymic triumvirate, on the contrary, had isolated himself from it and, when he felt part of humanity, it was a disconsolate part. Whitman believed in a cosmic plane, in a general order, in a destiny fit for all human beings:

> Do you see O my brothers and sisters?
> It is not chaos or death – it is form, union, plan – it is eternal life – it is Happiness.[30]

Quite the contrary, for Pessoa, and in particular for Search and Campos, the mystery of existence was terrifying and provoked a feeling of horror. The poetry of Whitman was tied to things, to persons, to experience and, less concretely, to dreams and hopes – but dreams and hopes in which the poet believed. The doctrine of *sensacionismo*, exemplified by Campos and Caeiro, did not require such an investment and did not derive in any way from Whitman. Pessoa had, rather, imposed the *sensacionista* doctrine on *his* version of Whitman. In section XIII of "Song of Myself", he wrote:

> In me the caresser of life wherever moving, backward as well as forward sluing,
> To niches aside and junior bending, not a person or object missing,
> Absorbing all to myself and for this song.

In "Oda a Walt Whitman", it is thus that Pablo Neruda turns to the Long Island poet: "entre los pueblos con tu amor camina/ acariciando/ el desarrollo puro/ de la fraternidad sobre la tierra" ["amongst peoples, with your love you travel/ caressing/ the pure unfolding/ of fraternity across the earth"]. Pessoa,

---

[30] From section L of "Song of Myself".

like Campos, did not absorb what he touched. He was filled by what he imagined. More than a "stroker", he was then a *voyeur*, but his voyeurism was essentially imaginary too. We have already broached the fact that Caeiro observed the world from a detached point of view (a step or a window). It is a tendency he has in common with Álvaro de Campos, Bernardo Soares ("Amo com o olhar, e nem com a fantasia" ["I love with my gaze and not with fantasy"]), the hunchbacked Maria José and the Baron of Teive. All heteronyms (and semi-heteronyms) are often themselves positioned close to a window from where they observe the outside world. It can be said, therefore, that "the speaking *I* is also a troubled *eye* that must be contented with the observed triviality of plausible reality alone" (Santos 2003: 18). Yet, Pessoa affirms with the voice of *Mestre* Caeiro, at times it is not enough to open the window to see the fields and it does not suffice not to be blind in order to see the flowers: "É preciso também não ter filosofia nenhuma" ["It is necessary also not to have any philosophy"] (Pessoa 1999: 186). With philosophy there are no trees, but only ideas; there is the dream of what could be seen if the window were to be opened, "Que nunca é o que se vê quando se abre a janela" ["that is never what is seen when the window opens"] (Pessoa 1999: 186). The act of seeing, therefore, is not a predictable immediacy. It requires an *un*learning and a dedication not only physical but also intellectual. On the creator of the heteronyms we may add, then, drawing on the words of Zenith: "It was above all *literarily* – through his invented others – that he gazed out a window" (Zenith 2013: 47).

Fernando Pessoa, just like the keeper of flocks, was "do tamanho do que vejo" – of the dimension of what he saw.[31] He was "uma placa fotográfica prolixamente impressionável", an endlessly impressionable film.[32] It is not by accident that, in a note from 1934, he pointed to Cesário Verde as one of the three masters of poetry of the nineteenth and twentieth centuries, alongside Antero de Quental and Camilo Pessanha. Cesário Verde, paving the way

---

[31] "Porque eu sou do tamanho do que vejo/ E não do tamanho da minha altura...", lines from poem VII of *O Guardador de Rebanhos*.
[32] Bernardo Soares wrote "Sou uma placa fotográfica prolixamente impressionável" (Pessoa 1982: 319).

towards "objective" lyric poetry, had revealed to Pessoa how to "observar em verso" ["observe in verse"] and had unveiled to him that "ser cego, ainda que Homero em lenda o fosse e Milton em verdade se tornasse, não é qualidade necessária a quem faz poemas" ["to be blind, as was Homer in legend and Milton became in reality, is not a necessary quality in whoever composes poetry"]. In fact, seeing (literally and figuratively) is all, it is the very essence of poetry – or, as asserted by Caeiro: "Mas isso a que v. chama poesia é que é tudo. Nem é poesia: é ver" ["But what you call poetry is all. It is not even poetry: it is seeing"] (Pessoa 1999: 270).

Presiding over the creative act, Pessoan seeing – as *voyant*, rather than mere *voyeur*, we insist – is also the expression of the author's desire to appropriate other poetic universes. The "other" became object and means of Pessoa's investigation, it became the window through which the creator of the heteronyms could inspect outside and inside the self. Either characterized through a chemical metaphor (catalyst) or a psychological one ("Grande Libertador"), Whitman, we are sure, represented for the Portuguese poet a crack, a fissure, upon plurality and upon the extension of the experience of the Real. If it is true that "[i]n the poem we read, what we really read is ourselves in our world" (Santos 2003: 61), Pessoa found in the lines of *Leaves of Grass* an encouragement to go beyond his limits, thus inaugurating a *dramatic* poetry, the most famous moment of which is perhaps the heteronymy – the *drama em gente*. The dramatic poetry, which was considered by Pessoa as the highest step in the sequence of depersonalization, was the expression of a poetic subject who was "vários poetas" ["several poets"] and who lived each and every state of mind "insensivelmente" ["unfeelingly"], as if they did not belong to himself, rather to the characters invented by him (Pessoa 1996: 106). Variety was, for Pessoa, the sole justification for an abundance of literary output: "No man should leave twenty different books unless he can write like twenty different men" (Pessoa 1994b: 208).

In fine, we may think of the dramatization of poetry performed by Fernando Pessoa as the releasing of multiplicity and, as a consequence, of the unrealizability of any synthesis. The refusal of any linear vision (derivative, filial) in his work and the elaboration of a literary project ever wider and irradiating in myriad trajectories at once is, beyond all doubt, one of the great proofs of the distinctive modernity of Pessoa. We may consider the gesture of writing differently, through contiguous accumulation, as a reprise of the conceptions that the singer of *Leaves of Grass* ("contíguo a tudo em corpo e alma" ["contiguous to all in body and soul"]) had of poetry.[33]

To be discontinued? Incompletion affords endless amplifying...

---

[33] A line from "Saudação a Walt Whitman".

Bibliography

PRIMARY TEXTS

Manuscripts and facsimiles

Rivers, Walter Courtenay. *Walt Whitman's Anomaly*. London: George Allen, 1913.
Whitman, Walt. *Leaves Of Grass*. London: Cassell, 1909.
Whitman, Walt. *Poems*. London: The Masterpiece Library, undated.

Printed texts

Pessoa, Fernando. *Poemas Completos de Alberto Caeiro*. Lisboa: Presença, 1994.
Pessoa, Fernando. *Poemi di Alberto Caeiro*. Milano: La Vita Felice, 1999.
Pessoa, Fernando. *Poesia Inglesa*. Lisboa: Livros Horizonte, 1995.
Pessoa, Fernando. *Poesias de Álvaro de Campos*. Lisboa: Ática, 1993a.
Whitman, Walt. *Foglie d'Erba*. Milano: Oscar Mondadori, 2013.

SECONDARY TEXTS

Alcântara, Maria Beatriz Rosário de. *Fernando Pessoa e o Momento Futurista de Álvaro de Campos*. Brasília: Thesaurus, 1985.
Allen, Gay Wilson and Folsom, Ed (eds.). *Walt Whitman and the World*. Iowa City: University of Iowa Press, 1995.
Alves, Teresa and Cid, Teresa (coord.). *Walt Whitman: Not Only Summer, But All Seasons*. Lisboa: Edições Colibri, 1999.
Bastos, Mário (a). *Paths Untrodden between Poetry and Philosophy: Whitman in 1860 and Pessoa*, unpublished manuscript [n.d.].
Bastos, Mário (b). *Searching for Walt Whitman in Fernando Pessoa's Private Library*, unpublished manuscript [n.d.].

Bréchon, Robert. *Estranho Estrangeiro. Uma Biografia de Fernando Pessoa*. Lisboa: Quetzal Editores, 1996.

Brown, Susan Margaret. "[Sem título]", in *Actas IV Congresso Internacional de Estudos Pessoanos Secção Norte-Americana*. Porto: Fundação António de Almeida, 1988, pp.35-43.

Brown, Susan Margaret. "The Whitman-Pessoa Connection", in *Walt Whitman Quarterly Review* vol. 9 n. 1, 1991, pp.1-14.

Brown, Susan Margaret. "Whitmanian Fermentation and the 1914 Vintage Season", in *Actas do II Congresso Internacional de Estudos Pessoanos*. Porto: Centro de Estudos Pessoanos, 1985, pp.101-109.

D'alge, Carlos. *A Experiência Futurista e a Geração de "Orpheu"*. Lisboa: Instituto de Cultura e Língua Portuguesa, Ministério da Educação, 1989.

Duffey, Bernard. *Poetry in America. Expression and its Values in the Times of Bryant, Whitman, and Pound*. Durham: N. C. Duke University Press, 1978.

Estibeira, Maria do Céu Lucas. *A Marginalia de Fernando Pessoa*. Doutoramento em Literatura Comparada. Faculdade de Letras de Lisboa, 2008.

Ferrari, Patricio. "On the Margins of Fernando Pessoa's Private Library: A Reassessment of the Role of Marginalia in the Creation and Development of the Pre-heteronyms and in Caeiro's Literary Production", in *Luso-Brazilian Review*, vol. 48, 2, University of Wisconsin-Madison, 2011, pp.23-71.

Ferrari, Patricio. "Alberto Caeiro and Álvaro de Campos", in P. Ferrari, *Meter and Rhythm in the Poetry of Fernando Pessoa*, 2012.

Grossman, Jay. "Martin, Robert K., ed., The Continuing Presence of Walt Whitman: The Life After the Life [review]", in *Walt Whitman Quarterly Review* vol. X n. 3, 1993, pp.154-160.

Güntert, Georges. *Fernando Pessoa. O Eu Estranho*. Lisboa: Publicações Dom Quixote, 1982.

Honig, Edwin. "Pessoa: the Way In and Out, through Whitman and Others", in *Actas IV Congresso Internacional de Estudos Pessoanos Secção Norte-Americana*. Porto: Fundação António de Almeida, 1988, pp.391-395.

Lourenço, Eduardo. *Fernando. Rei da nossa Baviera*. Lisboa: Imprensa Nacional Casa da Moeda, 1993.

Lourenço, Eduardo. *Pessoa Revisitado*. Porto: Editorial Inova, 1973.
Martin, Robert K. (ed.). *The Continuing Presence of Walt Whitman. The Life After The Life*. Iowa City: University of Iowa Press, 1992.
Perrone-Moisés, Leyla. "Un Futuriste Nostalgique", in L. Perrone-Moisés, *Pessoa, le Sujet Éclaté*. Paris: Éditions PÉTRA, 2014, pp.111-120.
Santos, M. Irene Ramalho de Sousa. "Poetas do Atlântico: as Descobertas como Metáfora e Ideologia em Whitman, Crane e Pessoa", in *Revista Crítica de Ciências Sociais* n. 30, 1990, pp.113-135.
Santos, M. Irene Ramalho de Sousa. *Atlantic Poets: Fernando Pessoa's Turn in Anglo-American Modernism*. Hanover: University Press of New England, 2003.
Zenith, Richard. "Pessoa and Walt Whitman Revisited", in Mariana G. de Castro (ed.), *Fernando Pessoa's Modernity without Frontiers*. Woodbridge: Tamesis, 2013, pp.37-51.

Consulted texts

Baudelaire, Charles. *Les Fleurs du mal*. Paris: Bibliothèque de la Pléiade, Éditions Gallimard, 1961.
Castro, Mariana Gray de. *Fernando Pessoa's Shakespeare. The Invention of the Heteronyms*. London: Critical, Cultural and Communications Press, 2016.
Coelho, António Pina. *Os Fundamentos Filosóficos da Obra de Fernando Pessoa* Vol. I. Lisboa: Editorial Verbo, 1971.
Pessoa, Fernando. *Cartas de Fernando Pessoa a João Gaspar Simões*. Lisboa: Imprensa Nacional Casa da Moeda, 1982.
Pessoa, Fernando. *Escritos Íntimos, Cartas e Páginas Autobiográficas*. Lisboa: Publ. Europa-América, 1986a.
Pessoa, Fernando. *Fausto* (org. Teresa Sobral Cunha). Lisboa: Relógio D'Água, 2013.
Pessoa, Fernando. *Il Mondo che non vedo. Poesie Ortonime*. Milano: BUR, 2009.
Pessoa, Fernando. *Livro do Desassossego por Bernardo Soares* (organização de Jacinto do Prado Coelho). Lisboa: Ática, 1982.

Pessoa, Fernando. *Obras de Fernando Pessoa* vol. III. Porto: Lello & Irmão Editores, 1986b.
Pessoa, Fernando. *Páginas de Estética e de Teoria Literárias*. Lisboa: Ática, 1994.
Pessoa, Fernando. *Páginas Íntimas e de Auto-Interpretação*. Lisboa: Ática, 1996.
Pessoa, Fernando. *Pessoa Inédito*. Lisboa: Livros Horizonte, 1993b.
Pessoa, Fernando. *Textos de Crítica e de Intervenção*. Lisboa: Ática, 1980.
Pound, Ezra. *Selected Poems*. London: Faber & Faber, 1975.
Tabucchi, Antonio and Lancastre, Maria José de (eds.), *Fernando Pessoa. Una sola Moltitudine* Vol.I. Milano: Biblioteca Adelphi, 2007.
Unamuno, Miguel de. *Del Sentimiento Trágico de la Vida en los Hombres y en los Pueblos*. Madrid: Alianza Editorial, 1995.

Index

Adam, 50, 76
Bachelard, Gaston, 32
Bastos, Mário Vítor, 18, 96, 113, 127
Baudelaire, Charles, 88-9, 104, 129
Brown, Susan Margaret, 36, 51, 71, 73, 75, 84, 87, 89-90, 94, 106, 118, 128
Coleridge, Samuel Taylor, 55
contiguity, 24
Eakins, 12
Ferrari, Patricio, 14-16, 77, 93, 117, 128
Freud, Sigmund, 103
futurism, 23
García Lorca, Federico, 117
Ginsberg, Allen, 14, 22, 37, 84
Hanged Man, 29
"Hávamal", 29
Heteronyms, 2
interruption, 54-5, 80
intersexuality, 40
Lincoln, Abraham, 80
Lourenço, Eduardo, 37, 39, 43-4, 56, 83, 95-101, 102, 104, 105-6, 108-9, 114, 117, 128-9
Marinetti, Filippo Tommaso, 23, 38, 43, 100
masochism, 43, 50, 105
Montale, Eugenio, 9
Negreiros, Almada, 104
Neruda, Pablo, 77, 122
Odin, 29
omnisexuality, 40
paragraphic rhythm, 78-9
passivity, 43, 52, 100, 102, 105-6
Perrone-Moisés, Leyla, 23, 57, 108, 129
Pound, Ezra, 7, 18, 34, 128, 130
Rimbaud, Arthur, 33, 87, 100
Sá-Carneiro, Mário de, 40
Saint-Exupéry, Antoine de, 62
Santos, Irene Ramalho, 24, 34, 38, 40, 44, 59, 80, 114, 123-4, 129
Shakespeare, William, 95, 105, 106, 116, 129
Simões, João Gaspar, 12, 37, 103, 129
Tabucchi, Antonio, 10, 13, 23, 130
Verde, Cesário, 115-16, 123
voyeurism, 123
Wilde, Oscar, 12, 115
Zenith, Richard, 14, 35-6, 106, 108-10, 113-14, 118, 121-3, 129

www.ingramcontent.com/pod-product-compliance
Lightning Source LLC
Chambersburg PA
CBHW060200050426
42446CB00013B/2916